HILLSIDE PUBLIC LIBRARY
405 N. HILLSIDE AVENUE
HILLSIDE, IL 60162
(708) 449-7510

Also by Tytianna

*An Exploration of African Folktales Among the
Gullah Community of the South Carolina Sea
Islands: History, Culture, and Identity*

*Sweet Pea and Sugar Tea's Country Family
Adventures: A Collection of African- American
Poems (Volume 1-4)*

*The Healing Tree: A Book of Poetry, Prose,
Meditations and Affirmations*

*The Bridge Kids: An African Heritage Family
Activity Book*

WHEN HIP-HOP MET Poetry

A Memoir By: Tytianna

Honey Tree Publishing, LLC
Louisville, Kentucky 40215
www.honeytreepublishingus.com

Copyright © 2019 by Tytianna N.M. Wells
ISBN: 978-0-9910318-7-0
First Edition- 2019 (paperback)

Library of Congress Cataloging-in-Publication Data
Wells, Tytianna Nikia Maria, 1987- When hip hop met
poetry: An urban love story.

1. Memoir. 2. Nonfiction. 3. Autobiography. 4.
Juvenile Poetry. 5. Poetry.

Cover Art by: Ashley Cathey
www.Acatheyart.com
Interior Design by: Honey Tree Publishing, LLC

Printed in the United States of America

This book is in memory of my daughter,
Nadia Michelle Robinson
*who was born an angel on May 19, 2005. May your
soul rest in paradise and your spirit live on forever.*

This book is dedicated to my mother (Superwoman),
Le'Donna Maria Smith-Arnett.
*I honor you and I love you. Thank you for never
giving up on me and always loving me
unconditionally.*

*You can make plans,
but the Lord's purpose will prevail.*

PROVERBS 19:21

*For I know the plans I have for you.
Plans to prosper you and not to harm you.
Plans to give you hope and a future.*

JEREMIAH 29:11

acknowledgements

A special thank you to the following individuals
who encouraged me along this writing journey:

God— the love of my life

My Ancestors

Grandma for encouraging me to write my story.

My Biological and Extended Family
(including friends, teachers & mentors)

My students all over the world

GLOW (Girls League of the West) Program

Anna-stacia Haley, Jonathan Udelson
& Quaid Adams

The cast of and contributors
to the song and short film,
"When Hip Hop Met Poetry"

Thank you all for being in my life
and blessing me.

author's note

One Sunday morning, a prophetic guest preacher called the congregants to the front of the church. I was one who came forward. He prayed over the church and for individuals including me—a woman he had never seen or met before. He gently touched my head and paused before speaking:

"You've been through what most people in this room could not have survived. You haven't told your story. Tell your story to more than three people. Tell them."

This book is my untold story. It is a collective body of work including a memoir, song/single (ASCAP), and short film. This partial autobiography details my life as a teenager from age 13 to 19-years-old.

The events and experiences detailed herein are all true accounts of my life as I have remembered them to the best of my ability. All character names and identifiers have been changed in order to protect the privacy, integrity and/or anonymity of the individuals involved in this story (except for my daughter, Nadia).

I began writing this memoir in August 2005 when I was 18-years-old and a freshman in college. The handwritten and typed poems in this book are original and unedited pieces that were written during my teenage years.

As you will read in this book, I have always aspired to become an author to empower people through my stories and poetry. I pray that my personal story reaches and blesses millions of people everywhere including you.

contents

'Read my book + if your
going through any of thes
bad experiances I trully
think u should tell someone
before it gets bad. ~~this~~ ~~stor~~
All of the poems in this book
are true. About me, family members, +
friendship, + expesally the pealpe who are in love.
Poems by: Tytianna Nikia Maria Wells

©: 2000 - June. 6
This poem journal is trully dedicated
to all that are straggling, doing drugs,
getting abused, haveing family problems, being
in love, Friendship, + has teen pregnentsy.
Take care + thanks for reading
my Poems. Love ya
Tytianna Nikia Maria W

Part ONE

Young Love

Tue story.

We were a real-life Romeo and Juliet. Bonnie and Clyde, even.

The whole world was against us, but we were inseparable. We were in love.

That crazy kind of love, too.

Real talk, we were the poster children of bad boy from the streets meets good girl from school.

And the story— well, it's definitely one to remember...

First Love

The heat from the Sunday morning sun was like a furnace in my Grandma's rust color, four-door BMW. We sat parked on the side of the street as Grandma finished a Marlboro Lights cigarette. We were headed to church but took a detour to my Cousin Robert's new apartment where he lived with his girlfriend Monique and their newborn son.

I was always excited to go to church, so I wore my favorite outfit— a white shirt, blue jean overalls, and matching cap that hooked onto one of my belt loops. As we sat in the car, the suffocating temperature was unbearable. I couldn't wait to open the door. My mind wandered onto the street as beads of sweat streamed down my face like raindrops. Gazing out the windshield, the heatwave made squiggly lines and ripples across the houses and cars.

"When we get out the car, make sure you lock that door, baby," explained Grandma in a soft and serious tone. She didn't notice I was melting in the passenger seat beside her, but I was spending time with Grandma, and anytime I was with Grandma, I didn't complain. We were thick as thieves.

"Okay, Grandma," I responded wiping my forehead with the back of my hand. I knew what she meant by those words. We were in the hood, and even though we were from there, we could never be too safe.

Grandma turned off the engine and strong-lipped her cigarette that quickly became a yellow nub. Slowly inhaling, a cloud of smoke filled the car and floated out the windows. The cigarette sat between two scissored fingers that held a long ash that only a chain smoker had the skills to make— that kind of ash doesn't have the courage to drop on its own. She took a final drag, tapped both fingers together, thumped the ash out the window, and exhaled. We rolled up the windows with the black knob that turned like a wheel, locked the doors, and headed out the car. As soon as we arrived at the front steps, the door swung open.

"Hey, Momma!" greeted Cousin Robert. He hugged and kissed Grandma on the cheek before turning to me.

"Whassup, Apple Head!" He grabbed me playfully for a hug and planted a hard kiss on my forehead.

After entering the living room, Grandma and Cousin Robert walked to the back of the apartment while I sat on a couch to watch a T.V.

show until my attention was pulled to loud voices coming from outside. When I reached over to the window to draw the curtain back, I saw three teenage boys walking in the street. Two of the boys wore oversized white Tees and baggy denim jeans that sagged to show their boxers. The third boy wore the same sagging jeans but with a black hoodie.

Watching from the window, one of the boys noticed me, made a joke that I couldn't hear, laughed with one of the other boys, and slapped hands. The third boy shook his head with a half-smile, did a special goodbye handshake, and walked up the front steps to my cousin's apartment. I hurried to pull the curtain closed and sat back against the couch before he walked through the front door.

He walked into the living room wide-legged, knees slightly bent, and hands deep in his pockets. The hood from his sweatshirt covered his eyes. I could barely see his face as he passed by me on the couch. No words. No acknowledgement. All the boys our age wore designer cornrows, do-rags, and throwback jerseys, but his style and walk told me that he didn't follow the trend. He lived in his own world and by his own rules.

Reaching over to a nearby table, he picked up a video game controller and plopped down on a separate couch to play GameCube. The simple jingle from the game was the only noise in the room until Grandma peeked around the corner to check on me.

"You okay in there, baby?" Grandma peered into the living room from the kitchen. She must have heard the door open. *Grandma didn't miss nothin'.*

"I'm okay, Grandma," I quickly replied to put her mind at ease.

"Alright," she said eyeing the boy suspiciously before returning to her conversation.

We sat in the same living room on two different couches with silence between us.

The boy didn't look up once, but I watched him carefully— his oversized Black clothes, the way he slouched on the couch, and the intensity in his sad, almond-shaped eyes— I wanted to know him, but the feeling and interest didn't seem mutual. I was invisible.

Grandma must have sensed how I was feeling when she said, "Come in here and play a game with us, Cuppy."

I had a lot of nicknames, but Cuppy, short for Cupcake, was my favorite. It felt good to be included after being overlooked.

We played the board game *Trouble* at the kitchen table. It was me, Grandma, and Monique, but when Grandma and my cousin broke away to talk in a different room, I couldn't wait to ask Monique a question.

"Who's that boy in the living room?"

"Oh, that's my brother, Rashad," She answered dryly. "He's staying with us for a lil' while."

I wondered why he was staying with them and not at home with his Momma. I turned around in my chair to get a better look at him. He looked like he was around my age but a little older. He reminded me of one of those bad boys from a thug movie that I wasn't allowed to watch or an urban novel that I wasn't allowed to read.

While Grandma and Cousin Robert talked, Rashad joined us in the kitchen but only looked at and spoke with his sister. They played the board game while I secretly admired him. Rashad was medium-sized, stocky built with brown skin, and a tough exterior. Just by the way he looked and talked, I could tell he wasn't from my world. He was from the streets.

After the game, Monique and I went into her bedroom to check on her sleeping baby. I couldn't wait to tell her how I felt about her brother.

"He's cute," I shyly confessed. I couldn't contain myself and keep a secret. I was a giddy 13-year-old girl. A new teenager with a crush. I mean, I had little crushes in the past but nothing like this. I never told someone that I liked a boy. It was always the other way around.

Monique looked at me in shock, "Rashad?"

I nodded quickly with a smile.

The surprise in her eyes softened and her lips shifted into a slight grin. The newness of the feeling lingered in the air until Grandma said it was time for us to leave.

Not yet, Grandma! I thought.

I didn't wanna go. My stomach was queasy, and my hands were achy from being nervous. Forget the flutter of butterflies in my stomach. I had an army of grasshoppers jumping in the pit of my gut. The feeling was new and overwhelming. I wanted to feel it all day. But when it was time to go, it was time to go. And I knew better not to question Grandma when she was ready to go.

As we walked back into the living room, hugged, and headed toward the front door, Rashad sat on the couch and went back to how he was earlier— silent, but I had a plan. *Typically*, when I ignored boys, it made them pay me more attention. So, I acted like I didn't care that Rashad wasn't looking at me and ignored him. But he still didn't pay me no mind.

Walking closer to the front door to leave, I wanted him to notice me, to look up, to show some kind of interest, but he didn't.

When we got into the car and headed for church, I couldn't stop thinking about him. *He's so different*, I thought. I hoped to see him again, soon. But little did I know, I wouldn't see him again until one year later. Not until the next summer break.

Yes

she had pain

sugar-cane sweet

Runs through her hair

Brightens her feet

Miss Goodie Two-Shoes

I was a middle schooler who followed all the rules and went by the book— the Bible. "Little Miss Goodie Two-Shoes"— that's how my peers referred to me. I didn't smoke, cuss, drink, have sex— I was a square in their eyes, but I didn't care. I had high standards for myself and was proud of my values and beliefs.

Following biblical teachings and honoring family values, I tried my best not to deviate from scripture and school. I was an honor roll student (mostly) who did as my parents said— I did my homework, read books, studied the Bible, and participated in school and after school programs. The poster child for the stereotypical "good" kid.

Although, I had perfected this outward appearance, I silently struggled with self-esteem and confidence issues. Images of beauty depicted in T.V. shows, music videos, magazines, and commercials began to influence the way I saw myself. Even looking at my favorite magazine— *Seventeen*— made me feel like I wasn't good enough. Being shaped like the models my age in the media became my ultimate goal.

Am I beautiful? I need to lose weight. I'll just skip a meal. These thoughts constantly flooded my mind— thoughts that no girl should have been thinking about. Being constantly bombarded with these images made it hard to see myself any other way. But writing about my problems helped me to better understand what I was going through.

My notebooks and journals doubled as a diary, helping me make sense of my feelings and thoughts about everything going on in my life including my day, faith in God, family, class notes, crushes, problems at home, issues at home, fears, and future goals and aspirations. These poetic entries were held in the private binding and pages of my diary and stored far away from everyone.

Side Effects of Insecurity

Looking, hating what you see.
People say you're beautiful
You wishing you were me.
Pain stalks into plunder.
As your conscious echoes thunder.
Thunder of pain?
Could you tell fact from fiction?
No & yes. You touch your features inchly
In the tall, lanky mirror.
Pain
Pain
Pain
Reeking blood. Your body. Blood seeks
Feeling so good.
Reversing pain takes over feelings,
The scented spill feeled me unreal.
And found my senses lost.
Using unfound energy
To
Cut
Cut
Cut
& hating yourself even more.
They stand picking you up
Calling you "beautiful" from the door.
And they still don't get it

Poetry: Jenesis

I was in the seventh grade when I watched the film *Poetic Justice* for the first time. That movie did something to me. Janet Jackson and Tupac were the main characters— a rare combination to see in the same film. Crazy thing was, even though it was a movie, just seeing them on the screen together revealed a deeper plot about how society viewed both characters in real life.

See, in reality, Janet was known to be a good girl and Tupac, a bad boy— a perfect combination for this hood classic. And just like everyone else who watched it, I fell in love with the characters and their love story so much so, that I watched the movie on replay. But not just any part— the parts when Janet recited poetry. I rewound the movie, wrote down the lyrics, and recited the poems repeatedly. I memorized all of the poems in the movie. That's how I learned to write poetry and perform spoken word.

However, although Janet was a great singer, dancer, and actress, she was no poet. But I didn't find this out until one day, I learned the truth in Ms. Davis' class. She was my Language Arts teacher.

"Alright class, settle down," said Ms. Davis. She waited for everyone to find a seat. "Today, we're learning about Maya Angelou. She is a famous African-American poet, author, and artist. We're going to read one of her famous poems titled 'Phenomenal Woman.' Has anyone heard this poem?" There were a couple of students who raised their hand. The name of the author and title of the poem didn't ring a bell for me, but I loved poetry.

"Great!" said Ms. Davis. She proceeded to read the poem.

As she read, the words began to sound familiar, and I recognized the poem.

That's my favorite poem from "Poetic Justice," I thought. I was confused.

Who's Maya Angelou? I felt bamboozled. *This whole time, I thought Janet Jackson was the poet.* Endless questions flooded my mind.

As soon as the dismissal bell rang, I headed to the car rider line to Momma's car and told her what I had learned about Maya Angelou. But I wanted to read and learn more about her and her poems.

"Can we go to the library after you finish doing hair?" I asked Momma.

"Yeah, after I finish, we can go," she said.

As soon as Momma was done working, me, her, and my baby brother got in the car and headed to the public library. That's where I learned about Maya Angelou's life and all that she had written.

With my library card, I checked out all of Angelou's books, but fell in love with her collection of poetry that included some of the poems that were in my favorite movie. While reading, I studied Maya Angelou's writing style. I took notes and annotated in the margins of her poetry books before I officially learned how to. It was a natural response to wanting to learn everything about her as a famous writer whose poetry was known all over the world. I wanted to be just like her.

One day, I hope my poetry is read all over the world too. I aspired to become a published journalist and author.

In each stage

I'm sad,
Welcoming rainbowed butterflies
Into my darkening closet.
My worn-through soul
Has nakedness pain
Negative deposits

I love,
Not because u loved me, but because
I loved u.
You welcomed me to gutter streets
And now I sing the blues.

I cry,
In time of furtive sighs
Joy is brief as summers fun
Happiness, its race has run

My pain stalks into plunder

Inspired by Maya Angelou

Fear of Darkness

I never thought my fears were in you

That you had problems scared of life too.

Every time I go home I am blue

I'm scared to go in

I wish I were you…

Misunderstood

       I was a normal teenager with typical teenage problems. I just wanted to be heard and openly express myself. So, writing stories, poetry, and songs about my internal struggles became my outlet. Journaling helped me to process some of the inner pain and led me to read the work of other authors who wrote about the same things that I was dealing with at the time.

       However, as I read books and watched movies about world issues, I began to shift my focus from personal problems to worldwide social justice issues surrounding race and inequalities. One of my favorite television shows— *Def Poetry Jam*, hosted by my favorite rapper and poet, Mos Def— used art as a form of activism to uplift the consciousness of its viewers. Inspired by the poets, rappers, and spoken word artists, I mimicked their writing styles and performing techniques. I was searching for my voice and hoped to one day be brave enough to perform my poetry on stage too.

       After countless hours of writing about my emotions, searching the dictionary for new words to use, organizing and memorizing my poems, and emulating my favorite poets and spoken word artists, I mustered up enough confidence to enter the school Talent Show.

I want my poem to really stand out, I thought. I skimmed through my notebooks and folders filled with poems until I came across the perfect one. It was a new and original poem about being Black in America. I had always loved writing about my personal experiences but in this piece, I was exploring Black history.

I was inspired to write the first of many poems like this after reading books by and about Black human rights and civil rights leaders throughout history including Olaudah Equiano, Harriett Tubman, Nat Turner, Malcolm X, and Claudette Colvin. These books were not selected in my school but should have been.

Despite the absence of these books in school, I continued to visit the library and bookstore to check out and purchase these books on my own. These books instilled in me a deeper love and appreciation for my history, culture, and heritage, that were visible in my poetic entries. Naturally, my writing evolved as I read more books, listened to spoken word poetry, and studied the fundamentals of creative writing while learning about the world around me, and my place in it.

***

On the day of the school Talent Show, I made sure to wear my black "poetry" hat slightly tilted to the side. It was only right that I had the whole look. It was my first spoken word poetry performance.

As I looked out in the audience, I saw Momma, Grandma, and my little brother Christopher smiling proudly at me from their seats. However, when I got to "that" specific word in my poem, I didn't hold back. I said everything.

Gasp.

It was the first time I used and said the word "Nigga" out loud. It was relevant but also added a shock factor to my poem. I knew just how to catch them. The gasp could have only come from my family. I had never used such a strong word that was in the same category as a cuss word, but they knew the values that I had expressed in the story about Black history was more important than being a "good girl."

Writing gave me a voice and poetry gave me courage to speak with conviction, the power to transcend my stories on the page, and the strength to inspire lives. That's when I became poetry.

Till Im Gone
U wont know me
never
deep inside of me
that Im hideing
untill I'v reached
a peek I wont
never be a comeing back.
The book of poems will
still be here
With all your answers to
your questions about me.
Im gone know
but the book is here
to take my place
while u read
I'm the person within the
writing I ame in the corner
of the book
I hold this book togther.
Since I am gone now & the book
u know who I am within t here
without u know the secrets...

Urban Love Story

It was a Friday night and Momma was working late at the hair salon again, which meant, I was home watching my six-year-old brother, Christopher. Momma had been working *all day long* styling hair while we were stuck in the house.

"While I'm gone, don't open the door for nobody," said Momma. "Even if it's family, don't open the door."

Typical instructions. She was what you'd call "overprotective" and didn't put anything past nobody. I guess it came from the danger and crime that she lived through as a teenager going back and forth from Detroit to Louisville. She wanted to protect us and knew the ugly side of life all too well. Momma was robbed at gunpoint, done wrong by people she loved, and left to find her own way in the world at a young age. She was determined that her "only daughter and son" would not experience what she had. She wanted more for us.

While Momma worked, me and Christopher always found something to do. We watched T.V. and played board games like *Candyland* and *Sorry*! And, when we got super bored, we used our imaginations and made up our own things to do.

Christopher played with his Pokémon cards in his room, while I pretended that I was a famous actress in mine. I sat on the corner of my bedroom dresser and made funny faces as different characters. I imagined starring in my own original comedy series inspired by *The Tracey Ullman Show.* That was me and Momma's show.

Other times, I sprawled out across my pink canopy bed with a book passed down from the hands of one girl to the next. It was my turn, and no one was gonna stop me from reading the new release— not even Momma. She would never have let me read those urban teen love stories had she known the drama and language in them. All my friends were sharing the juicy details of the book in the lunchroom and car rider line.

Books of all sizes and colors were sprinkled across my bed like candy. I had a lot of good books too, but that night, I was reading the newest one, *Flyy Girl* by Omar Tyree. Aunt Cynthia loaned it to me for the weekend and I was already halfway finished. It was a Black novel about teenage love. I opened the book, closed my eyes, and breathed in the paper.

You're not a real book lover until you smell the pages.

If the book was *real* good, the first two lines yanked me right from where I was and into the page. I was in the character's world now. The invisible best friend to the main character— the girl in the shadows of the book and between the words on the page.

The reality was the things the characters had— the house parties, boyfriends, tight clothes, and sassy attitude—I *never* could. I imagined swapping lives with the main character instead of being the invisible friend. I escaped my world through their lives.

After finishing a chapter, I closed the book and lie across my bed looking up at the ceiling. I couldn't stop thinking about Rashad. He reminded me of the bad boy character in my favorite books. There was something resting deep in his eyes. I needed to know him. The rush. The pull of his world— the danger— all so new and close. I needed all of it. But this time, I wouldn't be living through a book. This time, I would be the main character in this real-life story.

I picked the book back up, opened the dog-eared page, and finished where I left off. And after reading a couple of sentences, I was no longer lying across my bed. I was inside the book. I was in their world. I was becoming the main character. And that's when my life began to change.

Is it a Book?

People always wonder
Who is that girl?
Why is she quiet
reading
in her own world?
I hear their words
look them in the eye
I tell them what I am doing
I start to cry

They ask my why
I say it helps the pain
When I read it stops
the rain
So they look me in the eye
Tell me their secret
I give them their book
And say "baby read this."

That Summer

"We're going to Hazel Park!" yelled Aunt Cynthia.

We were at my Grandma's three-bedroom townhouse as always. Aunt Cynthia dressed her infant son Corey, while the rest of us finished getting ready. I had it all planned out. I was going to wear my favorite sky-blue short sleeved shirt, blue jeans, white bucket hat, and white K-Swiss. That was my signature when I was in middle school— K-Swiss or Reebok tennis shoes. That was when they were in style.

While getting ready, Grandma played the oldies radio station in the kitchen. That was our tradition. The rhythm of "Jimmy Mack" by Martha & the Vandellas filled the house.

As the music played, Grandma swayed back and forth across the kitchen floor, snapping her fingers along with the beat, meanwhile, the other hand dipped into her hip as a lit cigarette dangled from her lips. The summer breeze from the open kitchen window carried the soulful music and our voices out into the neighborhood.

While this was our usual kitchen routine, this time, we were saving our appetite for the family cookout. Cousin Robert planned the get-together with his girlfriend Monique and invited both families to a park near the river. I couldn't wait to go. It was a sunny Saturday afternoon.

Where else would anyone want to be other than grilling out with family?

This was the perfect way to spend the summer.

Aunt Cynthia and Tasha were fraternal twins. Cynthia was the oldest and was known as the most responsible of the two. I guess that's why she got a car first— a gold Grand Am. It was our get-away car to escape being stuck in the house on a sunny day. Wherever we wanted to go, whether it was to the skating rink, movies, mall, or park, Cynthia was the designated driver with me and her sister in tow.

The DJ was always the person in the passenger seat. Although we both had a fair shot at running for the front seat, my crazy aunt always beat me to the door first and got the job. We listened to our favorite songs on homemade cassette tapes. Aunt Tasha was known for making these tapes with all of our favorite songs recorded from the radio like Montell Jordan's "This is How We Do It," Xscape's "Just Kickin'," TLC's "Creep," Rob Base's "It Takes Two," and the Summertime anthem by DJ Jazzy

Jeff and The Fresh Prince— all 80's and 90's R&B and Hip Hop music.

Tasha was a pro at making these tapes. She put little balls of tissue paper inside the top of the cassette tape to re-record over the original songs. These tapes were all over the car— in the backseat, on the floor, and in the crevices and sides of the seats, but not too far from our reach.

"Turn on Humpty Dance next!" I yelled from the backseat.

"Aww, shucks!" said Aunt Tasha smiling, nodding, and playfully flailing her arms in the air. "Yep, that's the one!"

Tasha pushed the cassette tape into the deck and pressed play. While she danced in the passenger seat, I bounced with my seatbelt secretly off in the backseat where I had all the space to myself. We cruised around town with the windows down and the music turned all the way up. We sang along to our favorite songs that made us laugh and feel like summer vacation would never end. But this wasn't unusual for us. On any given Saturday when it was warm, you could find us driving through the neighborhood with music blasting from the speakers while singing for the whole city to hear.

By the time we finished listening to Side A of the tape, we arrived at the park and saw my

Cousin Robert, his girlfriend Monique, and her family. Cousin Robert stood over the grill barbecuing pork hot dogs and beef burgers. People of all ages were everywhere— sitting in lawn chairs under a tree, playing cards at a picnic table, getting cold beverages from a cooler, and talking over loud music coming from someone's car radio.

As I scanned the park, there were some people I knew, and some I didn't. Monique's younger brother, Rashad, was one face that I recognized. I remembered seeing him at my cousin's apartment a year ago.

Rashad was playing football with a couple of other boys in an open field of grass. I couldn't take my eyes off him as he moved. He weaved between the trees and parking lot to catch the ball. He was shirtless.

"I'm open. Hit me, bruh," directed Rashad to a guy who looked a few years older than him. He stood in the outfield with his hands in the air, ready to catch the ball in action mode, but, in my mind, he was moving in slow motion. Watching him jump to catch the ball, I paid close attention to his every feature— his tight chest, stomach, and the thick muscles in his legs and arms that glistened with streams of sweat. Well, that was until my daydream was cut short by the voice of a family member who yelled, "Good pass!"

While the guys played football, I couldn't help but notice that Rashad seemed to watch me in-between plays. I tried to hide my interest by turning my body slightly away from his view and joining my aunts in a conversation, but that still didn't stop us from sneaking glances, meeting eyes, and shyly turning away.

However, while lost in conversation and half-paying attention, Rashad caught the ball, ran toward me, and before I knew it, stopped directly in front of me.

"Hi!" said Rashad, smiling with the football under his arm.

Caught off guard, I responded with a soft-spoken, "Hi."

This was the first time Rashad had paid attention enough to speak to me. Aunt Cynthia rolled her eyes and looked away, meanwhile, Aunt Tasha gave him the squinty side-eye while sucking her teeth which I quickly met with a "mind ya business" look. As they stared at each other in surprise and confusion by my quick and sassy exit with this "lil' boy," Rashad and I drifted away towards a quiet place under some nearby shade trees before any questions could be asked.

As we talked about our summer, Rashad and I locked eyes longer than our casual glances. Blushing with a big cheesy smile on my face, my eyes were extra squinty, and my cheeks tightened like I had rubber bands stretching from one side of my mouth to the other. And everything was perfect until Rashad did the unthinkable. Before I knew what was happening, he lowered his head, grabbed the end of my untucked *favorite* shirt, and wiped the sweat from across his forehead leaving a wet stain.

Let's back up and replay that. *Did this boy really just wipe his sweat on me?* I couldn't believe it. I was in disbelief, but my face must not have shown it because he was still looking up at me smiling like he didn't do nothing wrong. I mean, don't get me wrong. He was cute and all with his *friendly smile, puppy-dog eyes, brownie batter skin that glistened under the sun*— but forget all that! No matter how cute he was, that didn't mean he could just wipe his sweat on me! If he was anybody else, he would've *caught these hands*, but I hadn't seen him in a while, so I gave him a pass *this time* and let it slide.

Consumed in our conversation, we lost track of time, and before we knew it, the day had gotten away from us. The orange sun was setting over the horizon leaving a turquoise skyline as a blanket of fireflies lit up the sky like lanterns and the sound of high-pitched chirping from unseen crickets filled the silent night.

I imagined Rashad holding me like how Tupac held Janet Jackson in the movie, *Poetic Justice*. I could daydream about us forever under those lights. However, my thoughts were interrupted, yet again, by reality— my Momma's tight-lipped and disapproving face in my mind's eye. I wasn't supposed to be having these feelings and thoughts! I wasn't even supposed to be talking to a boy. Our little crush could only be just that and through my cousin and his girlfriend's planned family events.

It would be months before Rashad and I would see and speak to each other again. Next time, the family get-together would be a wedding proposal.

Go figure. They fell deeper in love and made life a little more complicated for us.

Untouched

See me, oh, see me please
Your voice feels like the
Summer breeze.

Kiss me, oh kiss me hard
Leave your memory, bring a card

Touch me, oh touch me long
We say it feels so good, we know it's wrong

Love me, oh love me now
I wish you could, you don't know how.

Wishing you knew.

On Bended Knee

Cousin Robert had the surprise proposal all planned out for his high school sweetheart, Monique. It would take place at one of the finest restaurants in the city located at a high-end hotel on the top floor. The restaurant was known for its slow spinning dining room where you could see the entire city from the panoramic window view. Talk about *fancy*. My cousin was a class act and romantic.

We arrived at the restaurant, sat at the table for our first upscale dinner with Monique's family, and talked across the dinner table. You know, a few words and laughs here and there, but *not really*. It was awkward. Conversation was mostly between *blood-related* family. We didn't have much in common besides the fact that Cousin Robert and Monique had a baby together. Other than that, we were strangers who wouldn't have spoken otherwise.

As my eyes glazed over from the "small talk," I looked around the table and there he was. Rashad sat silently with his mother and siblings across from me. It had been a few months since I had last seen him at the park. I wanted to talk to him again, but that was totally out of the question.

Since I was not allowed to talk to boys, or have a boyfriend, I had to be extra careful under the watchful eyes of my family to not make it seem like I was interested in him. Since I couldn't express myself openly, I snuck glances at him. Finally, after a few seconds, Rashad looked over at me and grinned shyly. I felt like I was floating as my stomach fluttered. I quickly looked down at my empty plate.

The waiter arrived with our order— an exquisite dinner of fresh, piping hot food that sizzled on a decorated plate. However, while our family ordered extravagant entrees, Monique's family had another meal in mind— McDonald's. A pile of the infamous Micky D's wrinkled bags, boxes, napkins, and condiments lie spread across the dining room table. *Classy. Real classy.*

I later learned that after seeing the menu, Rashad and Monique's mother left the restaurant to order food that their family could afford. I guess you could say they were *resourceful*. But while one could see it as resourceful, another could see it as *Ghetto fabulous!* They had no shame in their game.

My Uncle Charles leaned over to my Aunt Tasha and whispered, "This is some—"

Before Uncle Charles could get a well-placed cuss word out, Aunt Tasha chimed in, "I mean, how tacky can you get?" It was a running inside joke that lasted for years.

Although our family couldn't too much afford the meals either, it was a special occasion for Cousin Robert, so we didn't ask questions. Instead, we just dug deep into our pockets to help make the night special.

Even when it came to the type of lifestyle we lived, the differences between our families were unspoken, but obvious. However, in spite of all this, Cousin Robert and Monique, still found themselves in love.

I looked over at Rashad as he ate his McChicken with requested special sauce and fries with plastic cutlery, carefully set to the side, if needed. Whereas, my highly ornate plate held parmesan herb-crusted chicken with mashed potatoes and green beans requiring handkerchief-folded silverware (insert double lip twitch here).

I thought it was *interesting* that his family ordered *gourmet* Micky D's and brought into this fine-dining restaurant, but I didn't let the thought linger too long. We exchanged bashful glances and smiles, looking at each other between bites, until our flirtatious glances were interrupted when Cousin Robert stood up from his chair, took Monique's hand, and bent down on both knees to propose. It was one of those moments that you could never forget.

Everyone's attention was focused on the proposal as they smiled, clapped, whistled between their fingers, and whooped. Meanwhile, Rashad and I focused on each other. Words didn't need to be spoken. What was felt, didn't need to be explained.

Wedding Bells

September 18th was Cousin Robert and Monique's wedding day. I typically wore my hair in pigtails, but that day, I was able to convince Momma to let me wear my hair down for once.

"Since it's a special occasion, I'll go ahead and let you wear your hair down," said Momma as I sat in her salon chair.

I jumped in the hydraulic chair and spun around one good time before Momma could say, "Don't mess up my chair."

She parted my hair and greased my scalp, running the oil through my naturally curly hair. I was so excited to attend the wedding.

I can wear my hair down, dress up, and go to a wedding, I thought cheerfully. Then, another thought crossed my mind.

Maybe, I'll even see that boy again. I smiled on the inside.

***

All the ladies prepped for the wedding ceremony in the dressing room— the bride, bridesmaids, and some family and friends. The bridesmaids wore red wine-colored dresses while the groomsmen wore black tuxes with crimson vests and matching bow-ties that coordinated with the decorations in the church. Momma styled Monique's hair, Aunt Tasha applied her make-up and painted her nails, and I silently admired Monique as a bride on her special day.

Monique looked beautiful in her white, off-the shoulder wedding dress that was adorned with sparkly sequin precisely stitched into the lace. She sat quietly and calmly with her hands in her lap as everyone talked loudly around her. She wasn't like the brides in the movies who were chaotic messes and crying all over the place. Instead, she was calm, cool, and collected.

I imagined swapping places with her.

If only this was my wedding, I thought. *I would slow twirl, holding the sides of my wedding gown and curtsy before walking down an aisle of rose petals to my dashing husband-Prince Charming. It would all be so magical.*

My enchanted daydream elevated when Rashad walked past the dressing room and peeked in to tell his sister something. When he entered, we caught eyes. I smiled and waved. Rashad responded with a closed-lip smile.

It had been months since last seeing Rashad. He was typically in a black hoodie, sweats or T-shirt, but today, he was wearing a suit. It was my first time seeing him dressed up. He had a different look about him— an air of confidence that I hadn't seen before.

Holding on to Rashad in my thoughts, I imagined that the special day was for us instead of my cousin and his sister.

Dang! Why did they have to up and get married? I thought. *Now, we will legally be considered family after the ceremony— but not by blood. Shoot! Had we met before them, then we probably wouldn't be in this pickle.*

During the wedding, Rashad's job was to stand in the place of their father who wasn't present in his and Monique's lives. They walked down the aisle arm-in-arm for Rashad to "give away" and present the bride to her soon-to-be-husband who stood with the other groomsmen. I had never seen Cousin Robert so happy and nervous as he watched his soon-to-be wife walk down the aisle.

While everyone looked at the bride, my attention turned back to Rashad, who slightly turned his head to sneak a peek at me. I glanced for only a moment, smiled softly, and held my composure. We played it cool, careful not to get caught by watchful adults, but it was nearly impossible to ignore each other completely.

Funny, how just a little glance can make you feel weightless. We were in our own heaven. A family wedding wasn't going to stop us from crushing over each other. Nothing would.

Reception

He looks so nice and clean-cut in his suit, I thought as we drove to the reception hall and parked outside of the red and white decorated building.

Me, Momma, her husband at the time, and my brother Christopher sat at a table for a plate of grilled chicken, green beans, mashed potatoes, and a sweet roll— typical banquet food.

Everyone ate dinner while watching the newlyweds first dance as husband and wife, and second dance with their parents— Cousin Robert danced with Grandma and Monique danced with Rashad. Afterwards, the wedding cake was sliced perfectly and served on little saucers.

"Now, it's time to really get this party started!" announced the DJ over the loud speaker.

Popular R&B and Hip Hop songs boomed from the speakers. You would have thought it was the wedding from the Black classic movie, *Soul Food,* the way Cousin Robert and his new wife were bumping and grinding to Juvenile's "Back That Thang Up" on the dancefloor— the unedited version.

It was definitely getting hot in there until Rashad jumped in-between the newlyweds, breaking up all the nasty gyrating and started dancing silly with his sister.

Rashad was typically serious or expressionless. He rarely cracked a smile or showed emotion, but when he did, he was careful not to show his teeth. He hid his smile by covering his mouth or lowering his head. Although Rashad was known for his "mean mug," no matter how he felt about his smile, he was handsome to me. Smiling, I watched him from the dinner table. It was nice to see him letting loose and having such a great time. He wasn't holding back at all today— for once.

Them Digits

The reception was coming to an end, and soon, only the volunteer cleaning committee was left— all family. They gathered and folded tablecloths and collected little wedding-themed whatnots and candy favors leftover from each table. While the adults cleaned, me, Rashad and his two younger brothers disappeared before we were recruited to help.

We escaped our families and sat on the front steps. We couldn't be seen talking alone so we brought Rashad's brothers with us. They were around five-years-old. *Bad idea.* They were what we called "Bebe's Kids"— snot-nosed, thumb sucking, bad little boys— to be exact!

Rashad and I talked about our summer plans, all the while, I couldn't stop smiling. Well, that was until I felt a gust of wind blow under my skirt. I quickly tried to pat down the fabric but stopped when I felt a small tug underneath. When I looked down, there was Nehemiah— squatted low on the ground, looking up at me, and snickering under my skirt with a runny nose. I quickly snatched my skirt from his sticky hands.

Embarrassing.

The other little brother, Josiah, threw his head back and giggled showing his missing two front teeth before sucking his thumb. They were bad as heck, but nothing was going to distract me and Rashad from talking to each other. It was the first time we had talked the whole day. Being forced to ignore his presence came with a lot of stress and anxiety of trying not to get caught.

Just before the reception ended, Rashad's cousin, James walked up to me and handed me a piece of torn paper. A phone number and the name, Rashad was written in pencil.

"He told me to give this to you," he said.

"Thank you," I replied with a shy grin. I quickly folded the paper, placed it delicately in my small purse, and looked out to make sure no one saw me. I couldn't believe it. *I have Rashad's number.*

Now, all I had to do was figure out when to sneak on the phone to call Rashad. I strategized and remembered I'd be at Grandma's that weekend.

Perfect, I thought.

It was easier to get away with "mischief" over there.

Missing U

I'll miss U so
but I gotta let go
& see u next time

Before we leave
I'll have to recieve
a kiss that lasts a lifetime

But now it time to
say goodbey
& see eachother the right

So
call me
dont tease me
lets talk at
night time

Sneaking on the Phone

I dug deep into my jeans pocket to retrieve the small piece of white wrinkled paper with Rashad's name and number written on it. The paper was folded in an endless number of ways to conceal the treasure— *them digits*.

The pencil markings were light and faded between the creases of the paper folds, but I could still make out the numbers by squinting. I smiled at the crumpled paper.

Luckily, Grandma has three house phones— a cordless phone in her room, a corded phone on the wall in the kitchen, and another corded phone in the back T.V. room.

I chose the phone in the back room.

No one will notice me, I thought.

Sitting in my socks on the carpet, I held the piece of paper in one hand and the phone in the other, feeling squeamish as I dialed Rashad's number. Knots formed in my stomach with each ring waiting for an answer on the other end.

"Hello?" It sounded like a young girl. Her voice was drowned out by loud talking in the background.

She must be his sister, I thought.

"Is Rashad home?" I asked.

"Yeah," said the girl. "Who this?"

I can't say my real name, I thought. *Think quick!*

"Tytianna— my name is Tytianna."

"Ra-shaaaad! Ra-shaaaad!! Somebody named Tytianna want you on the phone!"

A few seconds passed before I heard a boy's voice through all the background noise.

"Hello?" Rashad answered. "Who this?"

"Hey," I replied, lowering my voice to a whisper and looking around to make sure no one heard me. "It's me, Jenesis."

"Oh, hey!" said Rashad.

"Was that your sister?"

"Yeah, my lil' *big headed* sister," he joked like she was still close enough to hear him.

I imagined her rolling her eyes and neck while sticking her tongue out with her nose up-turned while saying something smart aleck— a typical little sister move.

"I had to give a fake name because I didn't want nobody knowing it was me," I explained. "I'm not allowed to talk to boys on the phone."

"Aww, okay," said Rashad, passively. "Yeah, I didn't know who she was talkin' 'bout.'"

Rashad laughed, and I giggled as we engaged in small talk. But before we got too comfortable, I needed to come up with a plan to make sure we didn't get caught. I had some top-notch spy techniques up my sleeve that I hadn't put into use yet, but with this phone conversation, I could put my skills to the test. I just needed Rashad on-board.

Basically, we had to be extra careful and on guard at all times while talking on the phone just in case we heard a click on the other end. If you have ever owned two home phones, then you know the familiar click— when someone in a different room, picks up the phone to eavesdrop on your conversation. We knew that any sound of breathing on the other end of the phone was a direct give-away that we had a meddler who wanted to hear all the juicy details of our conversation. The only thing was our conversation wasn't really all that juicy.

"I have an idea, so we don't get caught," I told Rashad. "If we hear someone pick up the phone on the other end, I'll act like I'm talking to your little sister. You just have to tell her what we're doing so she can know when to get on the phone."

We had this thing all thought out. It didn't take much persuading. With a little bribery from Rashad to a satisfied little sister who knew how to keep a secret by getting what she wanted, we were ready to execute the plan.

Our first phone conversation was a typical "get-to-know you" one. I did majority of the questioning though. I sat on the phone smiling and twirling the phone cord with my finger before asking my first question.

"What's your favorite color?" I anticipated the blue or red colors that boys typically liked, but he gave me something different.

"Black," said Rashad. "My favorite color is Black."

Huh? Who says Black is their favorite color? I thought, letting the silence linger before asking another question.

"What school do you go to?"

"I don't go to school," replied Rashad. "I dropped out."

I didn't know what to say. I was in shock.

"When did you drop out?" I asked.

"In the seventh grade," he replied.

I couldn't believe that someone like him existed. All I knew was school and *he dropped out*? He was the first and only person I knew who dropped out of school. I had heard about high school dropouts, but never about a middle school dropout.

Why did he drop out? I wondered. *I love school. I play clarinet in band. I sing Mariah Carey's Christmas songs for choir recitals. I can decorate my locker with magazine pages of my favorite singers. I'm going on a field trip to Disney World.* It just didn't make any sense to me why someone would drop out of school.

Then in my young mind, I jumped to the worst-case scenario*: Can he read? Does he even know how to write*? These questions flooded my mind, but I just didn't have the courage to ask him. I didn't want him to be ashamed if he answered "No." And, I didn't want him to be angry if he answered "Yes." So, I just didn't ask those questions and tried to keep things simple. However, I would later find out that he could do both and the idea of my questions became an inside joke between us.

"Why did you drop out?" I asked.

"I have to help my Momma take care of my siblings."

"Wow," I replied, shaking my head from side-to-side. I couldn't believe he was shouldering so much. But it seemed like a sensitive topic, so I didn't want to probe, and moved on to less heavy questions.

"What's your favorite food?"

"Momma's spaghetti," replied Rashad. "I like steak and meatloaf, too."

"I like spaghetti and steak too, but I can't *stand* meatloaf!"

Laughter erupted between us until I heard the shuffling of feet at the door.

"Somebody's coming! Gotta go!"

My aunt opened the door just as I was hanging up the phone.

"Hey!" I said awkwardly, trying to hide my guilt.

"Hey!" said aunt Tasha. "We're going to the mall. You wanna go?"

"You know I do! Just let me get ready, real quick," I replied.

"Cool! Come downstairs when you're ready," she said before walking out of the room.

As soon as she was nowhere to be seen and the coast was clear, I exhaled and laid back on the carpet in relief.

Safe, I thought. *Whew. That was close.*

I loosened my fist to see the balled-up piece of paper with Rashad's name and number on it. I smiled at the sight of the fading pencil markings before folding it back to its normal size and burying it deep into the pocket of my jeans. It was a prized possession until one day, it went missing and we lost touch, but I wasn't trippin'. Although, I liked talking to Rashad on the phone, I had new things to think about, especially now that I was a big-time freshman in high school.

Fresh Meat

Summer break had come and gone, and now I was a new high school student at the most prestigious school in the state. It was a privilege that I had definitely earned.

Now, I was a freshman. A big time ninth grader. And that came with its own new and old struggles with one being the need and ability to become craftier at dodging boys, especially, the older ones who were bolder than boys my age and had seemed to have taken a liking to me.

Fresh meat. That's what the older boys called us freshmen girls who walked up and down the halls to class. I felt like I was on a runway being scouted, or better yet, an auction block for sale. All the boys stood by the lockers watching the girls walk by and throwing out little words for any of the girls to catch. They spoke loud enough for me to hear:

"She's fine."

"How old are you? You are beautiful!"

Their little *flattery* phrases meant nothing to me. Empty words that just didn't stick. I let their comments roll from their tongue and into some *other* girl's ear. I wasn't hearing it. They were what Momma referred to as "manish" boys who attracted those "fast-tailed girls." I wanted nothing to do with those boys.

Momma always warned me about them.

"They all want only one thing..." said Momma.

Oh, here we go, I thought, turning my head to roll my eyes.

Even talking to boys, let alone having a boyfriend, was completely out of the question and that rule wasn't going to change any time soon. However, that didn't stop those boys from trying to get at me. I had my mind set on school and wasn't getting hooked to their fishing rod. Besides, I still hadn't forgotten about Rashad. He was riskier than the boring and immature schoolboys— a bunch of lames.

I mean, who just drops out of seventh grade and is okay with it?

I didn't really like that he was a drop out, but it showed me something different than what I was used to. His maturity came from all of the responsibilities he had as the man of the house.

He wasn't "manish" like the boys at school. He was a *man*. The real deal. However, as many times as Rashad crossed my mind, my desire for him seemed impossible to materialize. We just couldn't keep in touch. I was in school.

He was in the streets. Our lives were just too different. I had to move on. So, while many boys showed interest in me, I ignored them. *Not my type.* But, there was one boy in particular who caught my eye. Keith.

Hesitating w/ love

Do you like me?
Maybe love me?
Do you keep thinking of me?
Are you scared to tell me?
Are we friends or do you like me?
When you hear me, you don't speak
Hear what I seek.
Do you think I've moved on
Maybe, in love with someone?
Do you see me and want to touch?
Your dreams are filled with such.
As you watch me move real close
You act like you're a ghost.
When I stare, you look away
Yet, you wish that I would stay.
Can't you see me?
I'm right here
I wish that you were near.
I feel the same, as you
I wish that you did too.
But, I have to move on
I'm in love with someone else.

You're too late.

Finding the Solution

I hated math, but Keith made it all worth-while. He was my 9th grade crush.

Keith was light-skinned with straight-back cornrows. He had a rough appearance, but he wasn't a bad boy. He was smart, *sexy*, and *fine* with a capital "F"! He was on the football team, but he wasn't loud like some athletes— stereotypical jocks who craved popularity and thought the world of themselves as loud, obnoxious, and self-centered jerks. Those guys were always after me, but they rarely had good intentions. I wasn't interested. Instead, I was attracted to the boys who were quiet, smart, and unnoticed. That was Keith.

He was laid-back, easygoing, and stayed to himself. I liked that. Whenever I walked by him in the hallway or class, he always put his head down. His bashfulness softened his "tough guy" demeanor. He was rugged on the outside, but I could tell he was really a marshmallow for love on the inside. I wanted to know that sweetness.

Keith reminded me of my summer crush— Rashad— similar build and features. But Rashad was now in the past. Well, at least that's what I thought. The piece of paper with the faded pencil markings of his number written on it had come up missing and was long gone. However, the memory and feeling of Rashad still lingered. He struck a match and lit a flame in me. The fire that he started, on that hot summer day was still burning. When I saw Keith, the flame flickered.

He sat in a desk across the room from me surrounded by a flock of friends. I knew most of them. They weren't my everyday crowd, but it wasn't nothing for me to join their group. We were from the same neighborhood.

My circle of friends was small— girls who quietly completed their assignments, read the latest books, hung out at libraries, and wrote poetry. But as I worked, I couldn't help but look over at Keith. I was distracted and couldn't concentrate to save my life. I could tell he was in the same boat too. His friends stood around him talking and laughing off-task while he worked on "the packet"— typical busy work that teachers give students, so they don't have to teach.

I devised a plan. *If I go over there and join in the conversation, then I can talk to Keith.* Sounded easy to me. So, I made my decision, grabbed my math work, dipped out the desk, and walked over to the other side of the room where

Keith was sitting with his friends. I quickly joined the conversation, added my two cents, and everyone laughed. While his friends were distracted by the joke, I focused on Keith.

My little plan is working, I thought, smiling and drumming my fingers together while waiting for his response (insert eyebrow lift here).

He heard my joke, sat upright from the desk, leaned against the chair, and reached behind his head to fiddle with a braid. He had this big Kool-Aid smile on his face.

Gottem.

But he was still looking down at his desk and not at me though.

Dang. Look up. Say something, I coached Keith in my thoughts. *Oh, how I wish to expose my feelings that are unknown to the naked ear.* If only he could read my thoughts, but he was in oblivion.

Although I was taught that the boy should speak to the girl first, I couldn't wait any longer. I wasn't sure if it was me, or the little person sitting on my shoulder who always tries to tell me what to do, but all I heard was, *Make your move, Jenesis!* And that was all the encouragement I needed.

I walked over to Keith and stood in front of his desk.

"Hey Keith," I said sweetly. "Do you know how to do this problem?" I pointed to one of the equations on the paper.

Keith looked up from his desk at me. It was the first time we locked eyes. He looked nervous and caught off guard.

"Hey," he shyly responded, immediately looking down at his desk before continuing, "Yeah… you need some help?"

"Yeah," I replied.

Move in, I heard the little voice on my shoulder say. I followed instruction.

I found an empty desk next to Keith and scooted closer for us to work together.

In reality, although, I wasn't the best at math, I really didn't need any help with this assignment. I was a *beast* at solving algebraic expressions. And not only that, we were taking basic Algebra with one of the easiest math teachers in the school— the type of teacher who always has snacks for students and weekly movie days. But a little *damsel in distress* never hurt nobody.

I was getting pretty good at this. I mean, I was brave when I snuck on the phone to talk with Rashad, but this stepped my game up a notch.

Long story short, it wasn't long before I got Keith's attention and we made it official as boyfriend and girlfriend.

Mission accomplished. Access granted.
Problem solved.

Back to the Basics

Friday night football games were our date nights since I couldn't "officially" date. The football team traveled by school bus to home and away games where Keith played on the Freshman and Varsity teams. He was *that* good.

Keith and I sat next to each other, holding hands while riding the bus with the rest of the football players and staff. I worked as a Manager or "Water Girl" on the team. Basically, my job was to run water to the players when they were thirsty, caught a cramp, or got injured between plays. As soon as I heard a yell or holler, I was on-the-double running cold water straight from the heavy, dirt-stained Gatorade jug to players as fast as my legs would take me— I only gave Keith special attention though. His water had extra ice. *You had to have a certain level of "cute" to get this kind of treatment.*

Even though I cringed when he got a paralyzing Charlie horse while screaming at the top of his lungs in the middle of the field, or buried under a "pile-up," I anticipated rescuing my knight in shining armor on the "battlefield." This was one of the ways that I showed him that I cared.

"Ahhhh!" screamed Keith. He lie on his back, holding one knee while the other lie slightly bent against the turf. Keith's eyes were tightly closed as he rolled onto one side of his body in agonizing pain.

Oh, no— my love! I thought. (I was so dramatic at this age.)

I sprinted from the sidelines to the field holding a bottle of ice-cold water as though I was passing a baton in a track and field competition to win a championship gold medal. I would have earned a badge of honor for my efforts, at least in my mind.

When I arrived at the scene, Keith's limbs were outstretched on the field. I gently rested his head in my lap, all the while, I stroked his straight-backs and poured water into his mouth. It was a romance that could only be shared between us.

However, although our relationship was sweet and innocent, it was also short-lived. Keith was losing his edge. I was beginning to see him as a typical schoolboy. *Boring.* So, it wasn't a surprise that, by the end of football season, I broke up with Keith and traded my sprinting shoes for a colorful flag. Yet, I still was a runner, but for a different purpose.

The Sun is Approaching it's Rise

I stare,
Looking at the blinding window,
(the sun is approaching its rise)
7:01 is the time
Thirty more minutes, I murmur
Should I leave
Feeling insane
I can't really see or breath
Filled with energized energy
Provoking thoughts edge my existence
Excitedly hungry for the door of life
I grab clothes, money, poems and knife
My body halfway out of sight
(the sun is approaching the time)
7:30 I cannot rhyme
Still feeling insane in the mind.
The sun is approaching my rhyme the time
I cut and the blood is now blind
I write down a rhyme as I cry
I cry
I write down a rhyme as I cry.

Runaway Love

It was October 31st. Halloween night. While neighborhood kids dressed in costumes that they dreamed of wearing all year to collect overstuffed bags of candy, I wore regular clothes with a large black coat and hat. I was a teen runaway and it wasn't a costume. I was tired of the arguing. I was sick of being stuck in the house. And I was ready to make a bold statement to express how my home was beginning to feel like a prison.

I waited until Momma's customers arrived before I made my move. As soon as they went downstairs to the salon, I jetted out of the house before anyone could catch me.

Running as fast as I could, tears rolled from my eyes. The cool breeze dried my tears leaving white chalky streaks. My eyes hurt and burned from the gusty wind, tears, and fatigue. A mile later, I arrived at a church. I knew I would be safe there.

Inside, I used the public phone to call an old friend— Landon from middle school. I had previously confided in him about me and Momma's fights. However, this was one of the worst.

"You can stay with me and my mom," suggested Landon. "We have room."

As nice as he was to let me stay with them, the best option was for me to contact my own family.

"Thank you, Landon," I said. "I'll call my family and let them know what's going on and will let you know."

"Okay," said Landon. He was a loyal friend.

After hanging up the phone, I pulled my hood back over my head before walking into the darkness for miles until I found a "Safe Place" sign at a downtown grocery— a symbol of safety for an emergency. I just never thought I would actually need it.

When I entered the grocery, I spoke with the customer service clerk.

"Excuse me, ma'am," I said. "Can I please use the phone to make a call?"

"Sure, honey," said the woman. "Are you okay?" She had a concerned look on her face.

"Yes, ma'am. I'm okay," I lied. "I just need to call my Grandad."

"Alright," she said before walking into a back room. When she returned, she was holding a phone. "Here you go, baby."

"Thank you," I said trying to muster a half-smile.

I dialed my grandad's number and finally heard the soothing sound of his baritone voice.

"Hello?"

"Granddaddy, it's me, Jenesis," I said, rushing out my words. "I need help. Can you please pick me up at Grayson Grocery Store?"

"You stay right there, lil' honey," said Granddaddy Blaine. His voice was laced with concern for what he didn't know yet. "I'm on my way."

It was no more than ten minutes, when granddaddy's van pulled up to the front of the store, and I was in another "Safe Place"— his arms.

While sitting in the passenger seat, I told granddaddy everything that happened between Momma and me.

"Please, don't say anything," I pleaded with wide eyes. "Please, don't tell my Momma."

"Alright, Sweet Pea," replied granddaddy. His voice was deep, comforting, and reassuring. "I'll call your Grandma, so you can go over there for a little while."

"Okay," I said, relieved. "Thank you, granddaddy."

When I arrived at Grandma's, my aunts and cousins met me with open arms. They knew about the struggles between Momma and I since Daddy Kyle left us, but they never expected me to run away. While crying in their arms, I felt all the wounds open and weep with a new freshness. All I could do was feel the pain and cry.

"Don't Cry"
Knock, knock
wipe my face off
with a towel
to clear my tears
forever.
Coming
my voice cracks
with sniffles
snot clogged in my
throat.

I open the door
see my grandmother &
aunties.
I Burst into tears.
They were so happy
at first
know concerned
about me.

Tell me all that happened
"Don't cry".
He holds me.

Part TWO

Daddy's Girl

Flashback

I grew up with two fathers in my life. Unlike some stories, I had a close relationship with my biological father, Thomas. Even though he lived out of state in Michigan, we had a great relationship. We talked over the phone. He bought me gifts for birthdays and holidays. He wrote me letters and sent for me to visit him in Detroit and Saginaw during summer break. I loved traveling to see Daddy and the rest of my siblings and family. However, while these trips were fun, they weren't frequent enough and our time together was always cut short.

On the flip side, Daddy Kyle lived with us in Kentucky and symbolized fatherhood and manhood. Since Momma and I moved from Detroit to Louisville when I was two years old, Daddy Kyle had been a parent, provider, and protector. He had raised me as his own.

Growing up, we always had daddy-daughter dates. It was just the two of us.

After picking me up from school, we would get our favorite meal— a cheese burger, fries, and a banana milkshake from Rally's— a popular burger joint. We were two peas in a pod. I was his little sidekick.

Sometimes, we went horseback riding at the park, or to the track to watch the horse's race. I truly cherished our time together. He was my hero. However, the only thing that I didn't like about Daddy Kyle was how he looked at other women while Momma wasn't around.

I paid attention to all of the behaviors he tried to hide— the wandering eye, the double-take, the secretive ways, the late-night phone calls— the red flags of a cheater. My blood boiled as his head swiveled back to look at a woman after we had already passed by her.

Why is he looking at them? He should only be looking at Momma like that, I thought. My seven-year-old mind just didn't understand.

I wasn't sure how long our family would last with Daddy Kyle's growing infidelity and unhealthy habits, and this was just the tip of the iceberg.

An Angel in the Shadows

One night, me, Momma, and my infant brother Christopher arrived home from the grocery store. We were carrying bags into the house and needed Daddy Kyle's help, but he didn't come to the door like he typically did. Walking into the kitchen, the house felt different and the air felt heavier.

Daddy Kyle typically greeted us at the door, but he didn't tonight. Instead, he stood over the stove cooking a white substance in a small pot with his back to us. Momma spoke to him again, but he barely responded and when he finally turned toward us, his eyes were glossy and red.

Finally, Daddy Kyle said something to Momma that quickly led into an argument.

"Jenesis, go to your room!" directed Momma.

As I hurried to my room, the sound of heavy movement and footsteps made me turn around to see what was happening.

Daddy Kyle rushed towards Momma. She put her arms up to block him and fight back, but Daddy Kyle grabbed and held her arms down, striking her across the face, and causing her to fall back against the counter onto the floor. I had never seen him put his hands on Momma like that.

"Call the police!" Momma ordered. Her eyes were a watery red from a broken blood vessel that streamed across her eye like a bolt of lightning. Although I heard Momma's order, the trauma of seeing the abuse was paralyzing. My body felt heavy like I was melting into the floor. Everything was unfolding right before my eyes and I still didn't understand what was going on.

"Call the police!" Momma screamed.

Her scream broke the invisible hold that gripped me. However, as I searched for our house phone in its usual spot, it was no longer there. It had been ripped out of the wall, leaving a hole where it should have been. Immediately, I remembered Momma showing me that I could use the alarm system in the laundry room, in case of an emergency, to contact the police, if I ever needed to.

Momma's words echoed in my mind, "You're a big girl now. You need to know how to use this system just in case of an emergency— God forbid."

Back then, I never actually thought that I would have to press that button.

Running into the laundry room, I did what I was taught. I pressed the emergency button on the house alarm system. My mind was cluttered. Tears welled in my eyes as siren lights from the newly arrived cop cars flickered like amusement park rides in front of our house,— a creating a blurry portrait of the unfamiliar— a danger zone. Before I knew it, the cops were in our home, forcing Daddy Kyle's hands behind his back and placing handcuffs around his wrists.

Seven years old. I watched the scene from my half-cracked bedroom door. The flashing red, white, and blue lights from the cop car beamed through our front room blinds. The gleam created a thick fog that spread past the windows to spotlight up and down the dark hallways of our home. He was being arrested. Daddy Kyle was going to jail.

The house couldn't get any darker. That was until I noticed a small light growing from the far corner of my eye and streaming across the hallway from the living room. I shifted my focus to the direction of the glow and there she was— a giant woman who filled the entire door frame from top to bottom with bright white and gold ribbons that floated all around her. Behind her was a gigantic pair of white, dove-feathered wings. She was staring right at me. I had never seen anything like that before. Her beauty was stunning, scary, and unusual, but her presence was peaceful. Startled, I slammed my bedroom door, ran into the closet, sat under low-hanging clothes, and closed my eyes.

It was a real angel.

Moving Out

After that night, Momma planned to start a new life without Daddy Kyle. Shortly after, we moved out of our house and into a townhome.

Despite reality, I still had faith and imagined that Momma and Daddy Kyle would get back together. These thoughts came particularly at times when he visited us.

"Daddy Kyle's on his way to visit," said Momma.

Even though they weren't together, he was our father and Momma never wanted to take that responsibility away from him.

While Momma was cordial and straight to the point, when she talked to Daddy Kyle over the phone, it was a different story when he visited us. They still loved each other. You could tell by the way they embraced at the door longer than a casual greeting. However, while their friendship and love remained strong, what they had in the past was never coming back. Too much had happened, and despite the love that still lingered between them, when Momma made a decision, she stuck with it, and Momma had made her mind up. She wasn't going back on her word.

I had hoped Momma and Daddy Kyle would get back together and for everything to be normal again, but I wasn't sure if it ever would. I guess some things have an expiration date—even in relationships.

I want us to be a family again, was a thought that often came to my mind. I never said how I truly felt to Momma, but I didn't have to. She knew me like the back of her hand.

"It's better this way, Jenesis," she said, reassuring me after one of Daddy Kyle's visits. "He's still in our lives. You know your Daddy Kyle loves you."

However, while some things didn't change like their love for one another, there was one thing that did— Daddy Kyle's freedom.

Things Left Unsaid

It had been three years and we were outgrowing our two-bedroom townhouse. It was time for a more permanent move. So, one day, when Momma said, "We're getting a house before the New Year," Christopher and I were ecstatic. I was particularly excited because I was getting my own room and as a new teenager, sharing a room with my little brother who kept his side messy— all of the time— was getting old.

Momma had always been a woman with a plan. And you know what they say about a woman with a plan— she's unstoppable.

Although Momma worked all day at the salon, when she was finally off from work, we had family time and house hunting became one of our favorite things to do.

"Let's get some hot cocoa and go look for some houses," Momma said.

While listening to songs by Mary J. Blige and Anita Baker through the car stereo, Momma drove us around in a small, white two-door car as we searched through neighborhoods for the perfect home.

In the middle of winter, while sipping on cocoa, we looked through foggy windows that we used our fingers to wipe off to see the houses better.

Christopher and I took turns walking from the car to the plastic box in front of the houses that held a piece of paper with details about the property. We not only dreamt about our future house. We made the necessary steps to get one. She worked all hours of the day styling hair at different salons. However, with our dream house, Momma would have a full salon in the basement where she could work from home.

Despite her heavy workload, Momma remained focused on buying a house, and before we knew it, Momma was approved for a homebuyer's loan, and became a first-time homeowner, making our dream a reality. We were so proud of Momma— an independent single-mother who never let anyone or anything hold her back or stop her from achieving her dreams.

Christopher and I were naturally inspired by Momma's passion as a cosmetologist and entrepreneur. We hoped to be as strong and independent as her one day. So, we mirrored that same work ethic toward our passion and goals at an early age.

I was super involved in school and in after-school programs. I was on the Dance Team, in the Minority Teacher Recruitment Program, ROTC, and on the Ecology Team. I was heavily involved in church as a participant in our Rites of Passage program and a member of the Youth Choir.

Christopher was also busy working hard making good grades in school and playing Tee-Ball in little league with Daddy Kyle as the coach. Life couldn't get any better. Well, at least, that's what it seemed.

The street hustler lifestyle that Daddy Kyle had hidden for years soon caught up with him and changed his status as a free man. He was booked and sentenced to ten years in prison. Daddy Kyle was going to be away from us for years.

After he was incarcerated, Daddy Kyle's presence in our lives changed drastically. No more rides to and from school. No more daddy-daughter dates. No more trips to the barbershop. No more unlimited access to hugs and talks anytime we needed and wanted them. We were separated by jail bars, dorms, letters, miles, transfers across state lines to different prisons, tapped collect phone calls, staged photos, and restricted visitation days.

While I experienced Daddy Kyle's better years, my baby brother Christopher had to settle for his new identity as an inmate owned by the criminal justice system.

"It's not fair," I told Momma speaking for both myself and baby brother. "Why did they have to take him?"

Momma wrapped her arms around me and hushed my tears while holding my baby brother's hand. Hearing the kid-friendly and abbreviated version of what happened from Momma's point-of-view was heartbreaking. However, years later, when I was older, and she felt it was time for me to know what really happened to Daddy Kyle, she told me everything.

"Some things are better left unspoken," she said and asked me not to talk about it anymore.

So, that's what we did. We buried the memories, and never looked back. Yet, Momma couldn't help that she loved the man. Even after everything, Daddy Kyle was Momma's forbidden fruit. Soon after, Rashad would become mine. Like mother like daughter.

Forbidden Fruit

My attraction to bad boys grew after Daddy Kyle was sent to prison for his street hustler's lifestyle.

During his absence, it didn't take long for me to become attracted to the same street demeanor in boys my age. That's when I met Rashad. He filled the void of an absentee father for me. I filled the void of absentee love for him. We were both filling empty spaces and our relationship was built on those vacancies.

We were young, immature, and didn't understand the world yet. We couldn't have known that a structure with a broken, cracked, and uneven foundation was destined to collapse.

Like the biblical Eve, I ventured into a forbidden wilderness. Like Momma, I wanted this bad boy to be mine. I needed a thrill. I needed adventure. I needed something new. Rashad would bring that into my life and so much more despite Momma's attempt to protect me.

Overprotective

Momma was strict. And when I say strict, I mean *strict*. She was very overprotective. Although Christopher and I loved that Momma worked from home, it also meant that she could watch us like a hawk. I wasn't allowed to do *nothing*! I couldn't ride the school or city bus. I couldn't walk down the street by myself. I couldn't even spend the night at my friend's house unless Momma *really* knew the family. And, even then, I sometimes still couldn't.

"Momma, can I go to the sleepover?"

I don't even know why I asked. I already knew the answer.

"Who they people? I don't know them. How am I supposed to protect you if you are somewhere else around people I don't even know," explained Momma. Her voice grew as she continued, "They can bring anybody in their home and I can't watch you to make sure you're okay. You can't go."

Momma's words were always final. There was nothing I could say or do to change her mind.

She even had strict rules for the clothes that I wore or wanted to wear. I wasn't allowed to wear tight, or what Momma referred to as "form fitting" clothes because it revealed too much and gave me the wrong attention. I could only wear loose-fitting and oversized clothes that hid my "shape." Those clothes were not in style at all.

"You can't wear that because you are developing into a young lady," Momma said.

I hated that word with a passion—"developing." Momma was referring to my growth spurts of acquiring the round breasts that sat on my chest, held by a training bra and the monthly flow that required extra trips to the bathroom on the same dreaded month.

Thanks Eve for messing it all up for us girls (insert eye roll here).

I was going through normal hormonal changes that teenagers typically went through and I was embarrassed by "becoming a woman" and all that came with it. Couple this with being constantly oppressed under Momma's roof and smothered by her rules, I was beginning to resent her and think of ways to rebel. Even when Momma spoke from love and concern, I still didn't want to always hear what she had to say, even though it was for my own good.

"Listen baby, you are beautiful," said Momma. "Men are gonna look at you and you have to be careful around them."

I hated those kinds of talks. I felt like no man could be trusted.

"You don't want the wrong attention wearing those type of clothes," said Momma. "Focus on school because beauty fades. Your mind, your heart, your intelligence, your education— are more important than looks."

I grew up hearing these "talks" from Momma anytime she got a chance— driving to and from school, ordering food in a drive-thru, sitting in the salon, or parking to go into a store— and no topic was off limits.

One day, in particular, while Momma and I were in the car, she thought it was the *perfect* time to have "the talk" about sex.

Super uncomfortable.

Momma had a lot of wisdom, but this type of conversation always made me feel light-headed and claustrophobic. I slumped into the front seat as the car seemed to shrink in size while listening to Momma's long-winded lecture.

Momma offered blunt, harsh, abrasive, and brutal advice— straight, no chaser (I'm still scarred to this day). Her words stung. I thought the boys who I secretly admired and who had a crush on me were sweet, nice, and different from all the others, but according to Momma's general talk about boys and men, "He's just like all the rest" and couldn't be trusted.

I *hated* when Momma talked about sex. Whenever she talked about "doing it," a feeling of guilt immediately crept up the back of my neck. I guess, I felt guilty because the word was now in my thoughts. I was thinking about it— the forbidden word and act. The thought and sound of the word felt like I had committed a crime— like persecution. Like, I was standing before a judge and jury, or better yet, standing before God to confess my sins even though I didn't do anything.

So, from these talks and my own biblical understanding of the thought and act, I concluded that *sex* was a crime before marriage and I was *not* going to do it anytime soon without being married— point blank— end of the story.

Why are we talking about this? I wondered in the privacy of my thoughts.

The conversation continued even after going into the house. Momma went on and on about it. And when I thought I was safe to slide into my bedroom without her seeing me, she called me into her room where she grabbed her old, faithful, high school anatomy book. It was the largest book that I had ever seen about the human body and worse— there were photos! Extra-large ones too— *Ewwww!*

I hadn't even "done it," yet. I barely even kissed a boy. But Momma wouldn't stop talking and pointing at the pictures. I closed my eyes and made a face as though I had eaten a sour lemon. It was rough growing up in Momma's house.

Back then, I didn't understand why we were even having that conversation, but like they say, when you get older, everything makes sense. Momma wanted me to be a strong, prepared woman when the time came for me to face it. Her lessons were teaching me about the world and her rules were protecting me from the harsh realities of it. I just had to follow them. And there were a lot of rules to follow under Momma's roof. I was liable to get reprimanded if I didn't obey which could turn into an argument. Take for example, when I did something she didn't like, she would reprimand me with responses like:

"Are you trying to get the last word?"

"Oh, you think 'cause you got tiddies and hair under your arms that you're grown now? You ain't grown!"

"Do you pay any bills up in here? You live under my roof!"

"And you got the nerve to have an attitude."

"What you just say under your breath?"
"I know you're not getting smart."

It was always something. We just didn't get along. You know, that "teenage daughter and mother" rivalry. I did what she told me to do, when she told me to do it, but she never seemed satisfied. I just couldn't catch a break.

One day, I was upset about something and had an "attitude" towards Momma. I was also feeling brave. Actually, I was feeling froggy, so I decided to jump. I talked back to Momma, not realizing that I had planned my own funeral.

"You don't know what I'm going through," I whispered under my breath, speaking up for myself. On some level, I knew she could hear me even though I was afraid of the consequences.

Momma turned to face me, cut her squinting eyes at me, and drew her lips in tightly. You know, the "pissed off Momma" look.

"Have you lost your mind?" she asked with a crazy-calmness in her voice. "I *know* you're not talkin' back."

Then, she said that famous line that every Momma says to a disobedient child. You know the one: "I brought you into this world. I'll take you out!"

I sucked my teeth, rolled my eyes, and sighed under my breath as I looked from the wall back to my mother.

"Don't look me in the eye!" she said. "Are you staring me down?"

Dang!

I didn't know what to do. If I looked her in the eye, I was being "grown" and *bucking* up to her. If I didn't look her in the eye, I was being disrespectful. Either way, I couldn't win for losing. So, I just stood there with a blank look on my face, glancing at her frequently, careful not to be grown or disrespectful.

While standing in the same spot as Momma lectured me, the temperature in the room seemed to rise and radiate an aura of heat around the both of us in that tight space. It felt like Momma had been talking for hours, but it really was just a matter of minutes. All Momma was missing was steam blowing from her nose, ears, and around her head and it would have been the perfect portrait of a Momma that was about to whoop my you-know-what. I was ready to get out of there.

Like any other time, this one-sided argument requiring that I "stay in a child's place," always left Momma a winner. I didn't have a chance.

Finally, the "talk" was coming to an end. I could tell it was almost over when Momma lowered her voice to say in a newfound sweet tone that arrived out of nowhere, "You will understand why I do what I do when you're grown, baby."

And then, her most famous line, "You know I only do and say this because I love you."

All was clear now. At least from my mother's perspective, and I was able to walk back to my bedroom and breath in cool air.

Thank goodness that's over, I thought.

Exhausted from all the yelling, I picked up a book from my dresser and sprawled across my bed to escape into a different world. It was so much easier to imagine being someone else other than myself after those kinds of fights.

Poems
Helps your mind ~~get~~
get rid of your
disasters
at least &
for mine.

Write anything
Free your mind
& take controle
of your
writing skills.

Your writing
is at its end & you'r
wrote a whole book
expressing your feeling
that are dear to u.

Body Glitter

I'm just a child
don't look at me that way
I'm that kind of person
that goes out ~~to~~ play, play, play.

You might think I'm older
because my body has grown
maturely
I don't look at your body
and say those things
surely

So please I'm just a child
don't look at me that way
I'm that kind of person
that goes out to play, play, play.

Read, Read, Read
Read
Read
Read
that all I do
to stop whats happening
that is not
new.
hollering
fighting
arguing
I hate this much so
so all I do
is read
read
read
+ forget about my foe.

Read: Takes your mind off
of anything thats happening
+ its educational.

Part THREE

Secret Promises

Grandma's House

Grandma's house was my safe-haven. She lived in a townhouse, smack dab in the middle of the city where the business district ended, and the hood began.

My aunts, uncle, and cousins lived there until they became adults and moved out leaving Cousin Jada as the only teenager in the house until I visited on the weekends. She moved from Detroit to Louisville for a "new start."

Grandma's house was the place to be and she had it all. Cordless phone. The big screen T.V.'s. The piano. The comfort. The family. She also had the internet. While many families couldn't afford it and had to go to the library to get online, our family was one of the lucky ones. Grandma had dial-up AOL. The computer monitor had a CD-ROM that connected our home phone to the internet. We were living large.

On the weekends, when Momma worked super long hours at the salon and other jobs, and needed a babysitter, I went to Grandma's house. Cousin Jada was always up on the latest trends and teaching me something new.

"Cuz! You need a social media page!" said Cousin Jada, grinning and shaking her head from side-to-side with excitement.

"Huh, what is that?" I had no clue of what she was talking about.

"It's a site online for Black people to meet and talk," explained Cousin Jada.

"Oh, I think I've heard of it," I said, remembering a few people talk about it at school because they had a profile on there. But I wasn't too sure of how safe it was to meet random people on the internet.

"You're gonna looove it, cuz!" She slapped her hands together and threw her head back laughing. She continued, "You create a profile page and put a little information about yourself on it. You meet people from everywhere on here. See, look at mine." She scrolled through the site, showing me her profile.

I was sold when I saw Cousin Jada's page. It was colorful with pictures, fun facts about her, and background music. So, I gave it a try and created a profile. I posted a picture, my age, things that I liked to do, and one of my favorite songs— "Halfcrazy" by Musiq Soulchild. I couldn't wait to tell Rashad about my new profile.

Computer Love

"What's that?" asked Rashad with a confused look on his face. We were in the computer lab at the public library. I repeated everything my cousin Jada told me about a social media site, careful not to miss any details. Rashad listened with a serious look on his face. I loved to teach.

"Let me show you," I explained. Using his computer, I typed in the URL and logged-in with my username, *Jenesis_XoXo224*.

"This is my page," I said excitedly, showing off my page that took a couple of hours to create— I had to make sure my page really reflected who I was. I continued, "A lot of people visit my page and send me messages too."

As soon as I said that, Rashad's face changed immediately, and he perked up. "Make me one too," he said.

"What you want your name to be?" I asked him casually while the sign-in page loaded. Even though I just learned of the website, I felt like an expert.

Rashad looked away in deep thought and shrugged his shoulders.

"I don't know," he replied before asking with a slight stutter, "Wha-what do you think it should be?"

"Well, it has to be a name that's similar to who you are," I said. "Maybe use words like *street* or *black* cause you're from the streets and your favorite color is black. Then, it came to me. "How 'bout *Blackstreetz08*? The number eight can be for your favorite number."

He grinned, slowly nodded his head, and replied, "Yeah, that's perfect."

Having profiles on the social media site gave us a new way to stay in touch since we didn't own cell phones. But while we talked during the end of my 9th grade year, by October, we decided to "take a break." We still liked each other, I just didn't want to risk us getting caught. It was becoming harder to get to a phone and internet.

If Momma just let me have a boyfriend, things would be a lot easier, I thought.

It saddened me that we wouldn't be able to talk to each other, but not as much as hearing Rashad's reaction over the phone. He just went along with the idea without having much of an opinion and became quiet. I wanted to know how he felt. I wanted him to show his emotions, that he cared, and was sad like me, but he didn't.

As a parting gift, I made Rashad a CD with our favorite music, and asked my Cousin Robert to give him the gift.

"Okay, Apple Head," said my Cousin teasingly. He knew we were crushing on each other but didn't think much of it.

For two months, Rashad and I didn't speak. I was beginning to think maybe it was just for the better. But that would soon change with a visit to the mall during Christmas break.

Love Ghost

Because you are a voice to me
I lock my heart up with a key.

Because you are the beat of my dance
I will not let you have romance

Because you were there when knowone car
I told my secrets that you dared

Because you are to me
you see
You did find my inner mystery
But because you are to me
love ghost
You where the one I loved most.
   The love is gone

Playing Hard to Get

It was the weekend, but Momma had the evening off. *Finally, we get to do something other than stay in the house*, I thought. It was rare that Momma was off from work especially on a Friday. She typically worked 24/7 at the salon.

Since Momma had a free day, she wanted to go to the mall then have dinner afterwards— a typical outing for our family. So, me, Momma, her husband at the time, and my little brother Christopher visited the most high-end mall in the city to do some shopping.

After we walked through the mall and bought a few things, we went upstairs to the food court. It was noisy, but the crowd was dwindling down since the mall was closing. As we surveyed our options, there he was. Rashad— wearing a uniform and hat, cleaning the dining room section of the food court.

What is he doing here? I thought. I had secret feelings and still liked Rashad and was mad at Momma for being the reason I stopped talking to him. So, when I saw him standing there, I felt myself getting upset by the whole scenario.

Rashad looked up from wiping a table, smiled, and waved.

The nerve, I thought.

Momma recognized him. "That's Monique's brother," she said waving back at him.

Great, I thought. *Now, he's gonna think we're happy to see him.*

Momma was nicer to him than usual.

What's up with that? If she only knew that we snuck to talk over the phone, she'd be on my side and rip him a new one.

Since Momma was exercising her politeness, I felt I had to return the gesture. I gave him a quick wave, but quickly looked away in the other direction, careful not to give him too much attention.

Don't want him getting the wrong idea, I thought.

I was also careful not to show a change in my attitude towards Momma's politeness so that she didn't suspect anything. She was good at figuring things out. Thankfully, Momma kept the greeting short to browse the menu for dinner options. While Momma placed our order, I glanced over at Rashad. He was wiping the tables in his little work uniform, looking cute but I couldn't let him know how I truly felt. Instead,

I slightly rolled my eyes at him and turned away.
I didn't want him thinking that I still liked him
or anything, even though I really did (insert
eyebrow lift here).

We headed down the steps to leave the
mall, but once I got to the last step— my final
view of Rashad— I turned around to see him.
Then, before I could turn around careful to not
get caught staring at him, he looked up at me
and smiled.

Breathless.

It was the same feeling I got when he
spoke to me for the first time at the park. I
couldn't help but smile. While walking
downstairs to the parking lot, a thought crossed
my mind.

Maybe I should send him a text.
I did.

Text Message

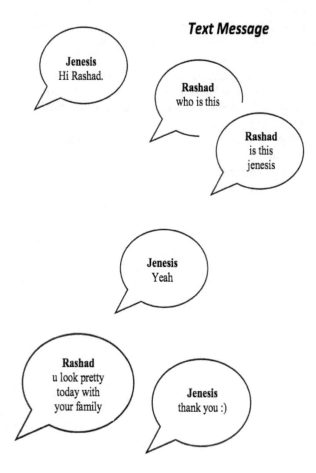

Shadows in the School

All it took was one text message conversation and we were back talking like nothing ever happened. I was in the 10th grade when we made it official as girlfriend and boyfriend. Since I was still not allowed to even talk to boys, Rashad and I had to sneak to do everything. And we were really good at it too. Summers off from school. Winter break. During school hours. After-school hours. Saturdays. We always found a way to be together. There was no place he wouldn't travel to get to me. We mastered the art of sneaking.

One particular day, I waited for Momma to pick me up from the old school building where I attended a youth program— that was where we met in secret. Everyone had left the building for the day except for me and a security guard who monitored the building. Momma was *always* late, picking me up between customers at the salon. But that was okay. The extra time made it easier for me and Rashad to see each other and be together.

Rashad often walked more than 10 blocks from home to sit with me at the old school. It was just me and him. Although a security guard was there, that didn't stop us from making the school our little "sanctuary."

We held hands while roaming the dark and vacant building all by ourselves. Our voices echoed through the empty hallway. Our shadows stood like giants hovering over us across the tall beige walls onto the ceiling. Whether we were walking the halls, sitting in the auditorium seats, waiting on the front steps, or standing in the school parking lot, we were there.

Even though Rashad dropped out of school, he still could have been in the program. I encouraged him to join. It was open to all teenagers, but he wasn't interested. While I hoped that one day he'd change his mind, I had big city dreams.

"I'm going to college to become a famous reporter and film director," I said confidently. I had it all figured out. I was every bit of 15-years-old and had my entire life ahead of me. I knew something great was on its way— God, passion, drive, and dedication would get me there.

Rashad never really had much to say when I shared my dreams and goals with him. Even though he said he was proud of me, I could tell my aspirations bothered him by the dark and faraway look in his eyes. I didn't know what it meant, but I didn't look too much into it. Rashad was not like the other boys around me, at my school, and in my programs. He had an edge to him that made him more interesting than the others. That's why I liked him so much.

"Can you backflip?" I asked Rashad. We stood in the back of the school building in an empty parking lot. I always liked a cute boy who could backflip.

Like most of the boys in the hood, Rashad could do the inherent hood shenanigans. To him, it was a normal thing that kids could do. But to me, he had a special gift. Kind of like one of those things that every bad little boy can do. You know, the ones who flip their eyelids inside out to show the pink flesh and red-vessels while chasing and terrorizing all the girls? I was always one of them, running and screaming, "Eeeeee! That's nasty!" But knowing if he could backflip was all that I needed to like him even more.

"Yeah," he answered nodding his head.

And that's when, right on the spot, he backed up from where he was standing and went into two backflips without using his hands to touch the ground. His shirt lifted up over his head, revealing his flat belly and smooth and defined chest. I was falling in love for the very first time.

How u feel
U look at me and want
to hold me
U touch me + u want
to kiss me

I touch u + u have
this feeling
its in your fingers then
shoots down to your toes
thats the way u feel
about me.

Its a good feeling
it comes only if your inlove.

In the Hood

Rashad and I met at our usual spot— the playground where he told me stories about being raised in the hood. I was captivated by Rashad's street lifestyle and the stories that he told. We were both artists and shared our art with one another. He would freestyle and rap on the spot for me. He also had journals and notebooks of his lyrics about what he went through and his struggles.

"Imma make it out the hood," said Rashad as he looked towards the nighttime sky. "Music is my ticket."

I believed him. I knew that he had the potential to make his dreams come true. Rashad just had to keep believing it. Hearing his music reminded me of my own struggles. Although, I was what Rashad referred to as "sheltered," I still had my own problems that I was dealing with and writing about. I often let him read my poetry in my journal and would read it to him. His songs and my poems brought us closer together. We understood each other in a way that no one else could. When Rashad talked about his childhood, I listened, held his hand, and traveled through the memories with him. Just like the books I read and stories I wrote, I imagined being right there with Rashad as he told his story.

Protect Your Hand

The game requires a player. There are guidelines. There are instructions. Even when trying to break the rules, there's still a certain way to do it. It's all a gamble. Your life is the hand. Your freedom is the bet. To be a good criminal, you have to be willing to risk losing everything. But what most criminals fail to realize is that there are no wins— only losses.

Due to no fault of his own, Rashad was dealt a bad hand. He followed the blueprint and was on a fast track to a life of crime. He didn't see any way around the streets. It just wasn't in the cards for him. So, he learned to roll with the punches and fought to survive, even if it meant destroying everything else around him.

Rashad was raised and groomed by the OG's in the hood. Like a mayor, they owned the block and made all the decisions. With a Momma on drugs, an absent father, siblings separated, and no money, the OG's from around the way taught Rashad the ropes.

They stood at the doorway entrance of liquor stores and apartment buildings like watch guards ready to bust a cap in anybody who looked at them wrong or had something "out of pocket" to say. But when the LG's or "lil' gangsta's" like Rashad walked through the hood, the OG's always had some knowledge to spit and wisdom to drop for the sole purpose of grooming the next "lil' Nigga" in the way of the streets.

"Maybe one day you'll take my place on this block," said one of the OG's. He stood upright like a tower with broad shoulders wearing a white thermal, black baggy jeans, and a gun holster. The OG fiddled with a trusted toothpick in his mouth while looking down at seven-year-old Rashad. Slowly, looking from side-to-side he spoke as his gold teeth shinned under the glow of the streetlight, "But you gotta be ready, young blood."

Rashad listened attentively, taking in everything about the OG that made him a "hood hero." His style. His personality. His posture. His talk. Everything.

"Always remember, lil' Nigga," stated the OG. "We survive by any means necessary, you heard me." He backed away, tapping his fist on his heart as a signal that the conversation was over. His words were a hood mantra.

When Rashad was in school, he was always in trouble— getting sent out of class, to the office, detention, suspension— he was a middle school drop out on his way to prison. So, while kids Rashad's age was in school, he was in the streets, and on his way to becoming a future criminal just like all the OG's responsible for making the block hot.

Bullying at school made him defend himself. Crime in his neighborhood made him protect himself. For Rashad, there was no other way around criminal behavior. He was a product of the low expectations of the people in his environment. It was his reality. It was his normal. It was all he knew. There was no escaping it.

While Rashad started with little petty crimes, by the age of twelve, he had a lengthy record— pistol whippings, fighting, stealing, robberies, selling drugs, break-ins, stick-ups, carjacking, shoot-outs, gang banging— you name it— all stripes that earned him bragging rights. He belonged to the streets and the streets belonged to him. And Rashad, well, Rashad wasn't slowing down or stopping for nobody especially since he was the man of the house and helping care for his younger siblings. He needed money quick, even if it meant selling drugs in his own hood to people he knew.

So, just as he was taught by the OG's, Rashad and his crew took up the mantel and kept a high supply of what the streets demanded for new and old addicts. Rashad was immune to all that the streets had to offer, and he was unstoppable.

On any given day, he and his "homies" dressed in black bandanas and long white Tees while cruising ten miles an hour around the hood in stolen, hot-wired cars with the music turned all the way up. You know the sound. When the beat drops, and bass from the speakers vibrate the street before you see a car turn the corner. When windows rattle and foundations shake like they are about to uproot. When everybody and *they Momma* stops what they're doing to turn around to see "Who's that?" That kind of sound. Driving down the street, you would have thought it was a block party or hood parade as Rashad and "his boys" drove around the neighborhood while hanging out the windows blasting chart-topping hits.

While kids Rashad's age completed homework assignments and anticipated getting selected for the football team, Rashad was preparing to graduate with a one-way ticket to either a grave or prison before the age of twenty-one. It was a badge of honor. A rite of passage. Something to be proud of— an airbrushed shirt with your name and photo on it, or news station with your mug posted on the screen for doing what you needed to do when you needed to do it. Whether 6ft in the ground or behind bars and whether dead or alive, Rashad had his mind made up about who he was and what his future held. A life of drugs and money was all that he really needed to accomplish the task. Well, that was until he got busted for selling to an undercover narcotics cop.

At twelve years old, he was arrested and sent to a detention center and boot camp for "delinquent youth" to help "straighten him out." The path to becoming a criminal always leads to failure. There are no wins. Rashad was about to find out just how hard he could lose.

Who am I? Why am I here? Why dont People Know I hide my tears? Why do you try to hide from your fears? Why do you leave when I came near?

Demons

We roamed the city at night. Tall blue and black skyscraper buildings lined the street, separating the business district from the housing projects. Streetlights. Secrets. Payphones. Runaway love.

We sat on a block of concrete in a vacant parking lot near an old abandoned, graffiti tagged building. That's where Rashad told me his story for the first time...

"Whenever we did something wrong, Momma made sure we were taught a 'lesson,' so she sent us to her sister's house— Aunt Sheryl. I got in trouble a lot, so I was always over there.

After getting arrested, I was booked in a juvenile detention center and given a case worker, shower, green jumpsuit, and one phone call. I called Momma.

'You're a strong young man,' she said. 'Don't be scared.'

Jail wasn't at all what I expected. Hood movies didn't show clean dorms and kids like me. We played dominoes and spades but as soon as I started getting comfortable, I was told that my stay was over. But the punishment wasn't. I was released from jail and headed to Aunt

Sheryl's— the last place you wanted to be if you got in trouble. Her house was pure hell.

Aunt Sheryl was a church-going woman, but she was no Saint. She had a dark side and wrestled with demons."

Rashad's voice trailed off.

"I should know," he said, lowering his head, staring at the ground, and rubbing his hands together.

I slid my arm under his, holding his hand. Resting my head on his shoulder, I listened closely as Rashad continued.

"I remember, one time, she tied my arms and legs down to a chair and beat me with a long, thick, black extension cord.

'That way, you can't run,' she said. She had the cord in her hand. I still remember how her heavy arms swung the rope over her head like a slave driver, whipping me. Leaving wide, purple welts all over my body.

Heavy tears sat on the edge of Rashad's eyelids as the pain of that memory resurfaced. He was back at his Aunt Sheryl's, reliving the abuse all over again.

Covering my mouth in shock, I couldn't believe the story that I was hearing. Tears rolled down Rashad's cheeks. Rubbing his hand and turning his face towards me, I wiped away his tears with my fingers and kissed his face. I didn't know what to say, so I said the first thing that came to mind.

"I love you so much, Rashad, and I am so sorry that you went through that— that's a terrible thing to experience and you didn't deserve it."

Rashad blinked away tears as he spoke, "We didn't deserve to be treated that way. No one does. She never treated her own kids this way but when it came to us— her sister's kids, it was like she hated us. I never understood that."

And when I thought the story couldn't get any worse, it did. Rashad went further into the dark depths of his mind, as he continued.

"Another time, I was released from Juvie, and on my way to Aunt Sheryl's house as a punishment.

When I walked in the front door, her orders were clear.

'Go get in the shower.'

So, I did.

After the shower, I turned off the water, pulled back the curtain, and reached for my clothes but they weren't where I laid them. Aunt Sheryl was sneaky. I knew something was up.

Leaving the bathroom, I walked across the hallway to my cousin's room searching for

*my clothes until I saw Aunt Sheryl over my
shoulder. She came from behind me, swinging a
thick, black extension cord above her head.
Running and screaming to escape, I grabbed
pillows for protection, but I still felt the snap
and sting from the cord until I crawled under the
bed and held tightly onto one of the legs of the
wooden bedframe.*

*But Aunt Sheryl was quick. There was
no escaping her. She grabbed my leg but
couldn't pull me from under there. I was holding
on too tight. Finally, after what felt like eternity,
she gave up and left the room. I was relieved but
knew it was only a matter of time before she
finished the beating. I wasn't going to hang
around for the next one, so I made my escape
out the front door and into the darkness.*

*After walking for miles, I found a bus
stop bench and fell asleep. I woke up to the sun
shining on my face, a bus ticket sitting next to
me, and a bus arriving at my stop. I got on the
bus and headed home to Momma's.*

Listening to Rashad tell his story, I
squeezed his hand as a reminder that he wasn't
alone.

"I wish I could have been there to help,"
I whispered in his ear. "If I knew you back then,

I would have loved you like I love you now. I would have helped you, Rashad."

Leaning over to kiss him, there was a sudden change in Rashad. He wiped the remaining tears from his face, adjusted his posture, and faced me. His head sat back against the thick trunk of his neck as he peered downward at me. His eyes that once held sadness and fear, were now layered with anger and aggression and had caught a wave too distant to calm. He seemed to search for something unspoken. In his mind, he was still in Aunt Sheryl's house.

I broke the silence.

"I love you, Rashad," I said.

I thought he would say it back like he usually did, but instead, he just turned away and stared blankly into the night. His eyes hardened and were stained with the pain of seeing things that he never should have. This was the hopelessness that life in the streets could only produce. It was the same look that he had when I first saw him at Cousin Robert's apartment.

"I guess everyone has their own demons," Rashad confessed, lifting his head chin-up. His voice was as cold as the bitter streets that had become his safe haven. "One way or another, those demons are bound to come out. It's just a matter of time before they shows up."

I sat next to Rashad with love in my heart and sadness in my ear. I wanted to show him that someone could love him the right way. I didn't understand his life. I didn't really know what he went through or how he felt. All I knew was that we were in love. We had that wild, homeless, unbreakable, limitless, dangerous, fearless— kind of love. It was just us. And that was all that mattered.

a friend 2 a friend

8/20

Beautiful baby,
listen to what I say
Dont worry
bought a thing
I'm always here to stay.

Talk to me whenever
about anything
to set the mood.
I know you & I care
you know
the right thing to do.

Never, turn yar back
on the one who lends the hand
I love you
& I'm here
I'm here until
the end.

When Hip Hop Met Poetry

Rashad was Hip Hop. He lived and breathed music. It was his culture and the language that he spoke. Hardcore gangsta rap always played from a nearby stereo— mostly West Coast rappers like Snoop Dogg, Dr. Dre, and Tupac. The melody of "Dear Momma" was often on repeat and religiously flowed where ever he was.

Cadillac driving, weed smoking, sippin' on that "Yak," grilling in the front courtyard, sitting back and watching people walk by— a typical day in the hood. That was his world. Rashad was the music, and while he was Hip Hop, I was poetry.

We shared the same passion for writing. He wrote rap lyrics. I wrote poetry. He wrote the verse. I wrote the flow. Although we shared the same love for writing, we had different tastes in music. I listened to conscious rap— East Coast rappers like Mos Def, Common, The Roots, and Talib Kweli.

Our musical choices showed a difference in our worlds, but we introduced each other to the message and created our own story.

Inferno

Rashad was my real life, roughneck, bad boy. He wasn't a school boy who pretended to be street. Rashad was from the hood. He survived it every day. His decision to get a nose ring inspired by his favorite rapper— Tupac— was evidence.

While I was in school following all the rules, Rashad was on the street corner and alleys slangin' drugs, gang bangin', and breaking every rule he could in order to get what he wanted— quick money.

While I was exchanging books from one friend to the next, Rashad was on the block exchanging small bags of dope from one fiend to the next. No one would have ever expected us to find each other, let alone, be together. I guess it's true: opposites attract. The forbiddenness of our relationship was what kept the fire burning.

People around us continually tried to snuff out our flame, but their comments acted as gasoline further igniting our passion for one another. We were total opposites and that's what made our young love such a fire hazard.

R + J

We sometimes met at a railroad track that ran through the neighborhood on a dead-end street. Our spot of choice— a crossroads— would unknowingly become a metaphor for our lives.

Rashad tagged our name in graffiti on a brick wall by the train tracks that became one of our many hiding places. While walking along the grimy tracks between streetlights surrounded by halos of gnats and mosquitoes, we envisioned our future together. We were lost in love and time and that's the way we wanted it. However, the crossroads were an undeniable reminder that if anyone found out about us, there would be hell to pay.

Although, we really didn't care what anyone on the outside thought about us, my family was a different story. I feared my religious mother's reaction. She always said, "everything in the dark will come to light."

Leaning deeper into Rashad, I tried to ignore the sickening feeling in my stomach of being caught. However, in the back of my mind, I couldn't help but wonder, if it was only a matter of time before a spotlight exposed our relationship, revealing everything we tried to hide. I hoped our love wouldn't be like the street— a dead end.

Missing You

Our sneaky behavior didn't stop there. One particular weekend, I visited Aunt Cynthia and her five-year-old son at their new apartment. She lived across the street from Rashad. Since my aunt had moved, sneaking on the phone to talk to Rashad became a lot easier. After a while of talking secretly, it wasn't enough anymore. We wanted to see each other.

"I miss you," said Rashad over the phone.

Butterflies awakened deep in my stomach.

"I miss you too," I replied, blushing as an idea came to me.

Aunt Cynthia works the nightshift, so we can see each other while she's gone... I thought. So, I shared the plan with Rashad.

"When my aunt goes to work, you can come over," I said confidently, "But you can't come inside the apartment."

Even though I made the plan, I was still uneasy about it, as I thought of the repercussions.

My aunt will have a hissy fit— a total conniption, if she knew I was with a boy, let alone, had one over her house. I could only imagine.

As nervousness about our plan set in, I thought of all the things that could go wrong. I was so nervous to bring a boy over, let alone, a boy over to my aunt's apartment. Although he wasn't coming in, I still felt guilty for bringing him over without her consent. I had never done anything like this before. So, I thought long and hard about the consequences and had another idea.

"Instead, let's just meet at the neighborhood park," I said. "But we can't stay long."

Rashad agreed.

***

Later that night, a few hours after Aunt Cynthia left for work, I made my way over to the park to meet Rashad. Although I wasn't supposed to leave the apartment for any reason, I had to see him. This would be our first real meet-up without the company of adults.

In the depths of the early morning darkness, I walked towards the playground in the park as the sound of thousands of crickets filled the silence with their music. And just between the shadows of the tree limbs and under the dimness of the park lights, I finally saw him. I wanted to run into his arms like what I saw in romantic movies, but I held my cool for the time being.

As we walked closer to each other, my heart raced. Pulling me into a tight hug, all of my anxieties about us meeting vanished. We were finally together alone and away from everyone. Just us. Rashad's arms were safe, warm, and strong. Our love was raw and open. Vibrant and new.

Young Love

The white glow of the midnight moon lit up the playground. Dark shadows covered the bridge and monkey bars, hiding and protecting our forbidden love.

Rashad and I found a spot at the top of the slide where we sat hand-in-hand talking in the refuge of the darkness. Cars were parked. Apartment lights were off. The streets were lonely as the gentle whistle of the night breeze blew around us, but we had each other. We were so lost in the night together that we didn't realize how late it was getting.

The sun was rising. It was *way* past my bedtime even before I got to the playground. I wanted to stay but I knew I had to get back to the apartment before my aunt got there.

"I better be heading back," I shyly said to Rashad.

While leaving the park, hand-in-hand, Rashad swiveled his body toward me unexpectedly, speaking in one breath as though he had been holding in his words.

"I'm in love with you, Jenesis," he confessed.

This was my first time hearing him say those words. Rashad delicately caressed my face and drew me in close for a deep and passionate kiss. His body was warm. My body was weightless.

"I'm in love with you too, Rashad," I replied.

We held each other with so many words unspoken, but I could feel each one like electricity flowing through my body. I was playing with fire and falling in love all at the same time.

Irresistible

I sit on my porch
cars + people stare at me
I look around to wonder
what is it ~~that~~ they see.
I walk into the room
as jazz ~~moves through my feet~~ ~~●●●~~ ~~●●●●●~~
the men swarm around me
a ~~●~~ hive of honeybees.
They say I've got ~~that~~ glow
~~that~~ beauty in me
~~they~~ say that I am art
~~●●●●●●●●●●●●●●●●●~~ I have an air of mystery
~~they~~ fall down at my knees
~~they~~ kiss my feet
cause never once in all their lives
had known a girl like me.

148

A Midnight Kiss

The next afternoon, I couldn't wait to talk with Rashad. As soon as I had the opportunity, I snuck away to call him from Aunt Cynthia's bedroom phone. The coast was clear since she was cooking in the kitchen.

"I wanna see you again, Pretty," he said.

"Me too," I said smiling while lying in my aunt's bed.

I knew that Aunt Cynthia was working the nightshift again and I really wanted to see Rashad like last night. So, that's what we did.

***

When we met early the next morning, the sky was a sleepy blue haze. Standing in silence, we tightly held each other behind the fenced-in backyard of my aunt's apartment. My head resting against his chiseled chest. His chin resting at the top of my head. Our heartbeats in sync. I felt the calm pace of Rashad's pulse increase before he spoke.

"Here," he said, holding a brown paper bag in his hand that I hadn't realized he was holding. "I got you somethin'."

Looking in the bag, I pulled out my all-time favorite morning snacks— a cold glass of fresh orange juice and two sweet muffins.

"Thank you!" I said smiling. He always made me feel so special.

We shared our muffins and talked until Rashad's cell phone rang. Reaching into his pocket, he answered his phone and walked closer to the fence to talk.

Drinking my orange juice, I listened to Rashad's conversation but couldn't make out the language. He was speaking in code. Unbeknownst to me at the time, I would later learn that he also spoke another language— "Street." The conversation only lasted a couple of seconds, before Rashad ended the call and turned toward me.

"I gotta make this run real quick," he said. His toboggan sat above his eyes making them look lower than normal. His hands dug deep into the pockets of his sweatpants. "They waitin' on me."

I was confused.

"Where are you going?" I asked, unable to hide the worry in my voice.

Rashad looked away while squinting his eyes and sucking his teeth.

But I already knew the answer by putting two and two together. I just wanted him to tell me himself. So, instead of asking him more questions, I tried something different.

"Let me see what it looks like," I asked bravely with my arms folded.

Rashad looked back at me with a straight face. He hesitated for a few seconds before reaching into his pocket and pulling out a small zip lock bag of a substance that looked like broken white crystal-rocks. That was the first time I saw crack.

Caught Up: Being in the Hood shot

The beat,
screamed the calls
of hatred.
Unwondering existendes
wandered for my soul.
Wanting me to call,
call & pump my legs
past and even fast
to the cement,
while my head begins
to swell
& my eyes
roll, self-cantiously or
vigiarsly
behind the black.
And I cry,
my surrounding's
pressure me,
crying to me.
~~so~~ My life is being
drowned by
the scenery

152

Life Choices

I was an honor roll student. Meanwhile, Rashad was making money by his own terms.

"I don't want you selling drugs," I confided in him. "That's somebody's family member out there you're selling to. It's just not right."

"I understand where you comin' from, baby," Rashad said. "But we're from two different worlds, and I need the money to survive. Plus, I should be providin' for you."

"Nothing good is gonna come from it," I said. "Stop selling and go back to school to get your GED."

But Rashad wasn't hearing all that. He was still knee-deep in the trenches and no one was going to redirect his path.

"All my homies I grew up with are either locked up, dead, or in jail," explained Rashad. "There ain't too many options out here for a Nigga like me, baby."

I listened as he continued.

"Ain't nothin' 'round me but poor Black people struggling to make it. I gotta help take care of my siblings. Nobody else is gonna do it. This is my life. This is my reality." He paused before continuing, "And I ain't going back to school. Maybe one day, but I need to eat, and we need to live."

I didn't know what else to say. I hated when Rashad talked like this, but he was right. Everyone around him was getting busted or buried. I needed him to hear me, but he had his mind made up and I couldn't change it.

"I don't want you living this type of life, Rashad."

"This life chose me," he replied looking away.

I slid my hand gently against the side of his face before speaking, "It's dangerous out there and I just don't want nothin' to happen to you," I said. "I don't want you to get hurt or in trouble," I explained.

"Listen," said Rashad, taking my hands into his and looking into my eyes. He always did everything with so much heart. "I love you," he said. Sighing, he shook his head and looked down at our hands before continuing. "I love you so much. And... I'm gonna do everything I possibly can to make you happy, baby... But right now, this is what I gotta do."

Rashad still wasn't listening to me. As I looked away, shaking my head in disbelief, Rashad spoke clearly.

"Baby, nothin's gonna happen to me. Nothin'. I promise. You hear me?"

Swallowing my uncertainty, the best way I could, and holding back my tears, I looked into Rashad's eyes and confidently responded, "Yes."

Rashad hugged me tightly before holding my face in his hands, kissing away my tears, and meeting my lips with his. We had so much hope and faith in our love.

Cruising

We rode 15-speed bikes. It was our only transportation option. We didn't have a driver's permit or license, and we definitely didn't have a car, but we had love. And, that love took us all over the city. We had that limitless kind of love.

Every time Rashad and I met, he seemed to have a different— a cheap-looking bike with chipped paint and a rusted chain that contrasted with mine. I had one of those nice, expensive cruisers with a basket attached.

"Where'd you get your bike?" I asked Rashad before we started our trail.

He never really told me outright that he stole the bike, but that's what he did. If he saw one just parked without an owner or lock, he took it for his own.

"I found it around the way," he said, nonchalantly.

I thought it was odd but left it at that and didn't ask any more questions. I was just happy that he had a bike, so we could have fun.

We slow pedaled side-by-side and hand-in-hand at the same speed through different hoods. Rashad was a daredevil. He could ride his bike hands-free down to his sides while looking at me smiling. He was always doing something dangerous.

I wanted to try, too.

"Watch me!" I said, imitating Rashad.

When I let go of the handle bars for a few seconds, my bike wobbled and veered off to the side. Catching my balance, I quickly grabbed the handle bars. It was an epic fail.

We explored all that the city had to offer for hours, until the street lights turned on and the lightning bugs floated in the blue night. We found ourselves lost in each other. Careful not to ride too close to the main streets, for someone to recognize us, we took the backroads near old train tracks and industrial zones. It was freedom. We were finally liberated from all the rules, expectations, and limitations. We were in our own world.

When we weren't riding our bikes, we roamed the city by foot. Walking granted us access to the city's most forbidden areas— secluded and forgotten about playgrounds, abandoned schools, fire escapes on the outside of buildings, hidden stairwells, vacant library rooms, doors that had been accidently unlocked— places where we knew no one would find us.

Rashad was the bad boy I always wanted. I called him a *thug*.

He laughed before correcting me and referred to himself as "street."

"It's the *same* thing," I said scrunching up my nose, shrugging my shoulders, and shaking my head.

"There's a difference," he explained matter-of-factly and enunciating each syllable like he never did.

Debates like this were typical of our conversations being that we were from two different worlds.

I sighed, rolling my eyes with a half-smile. "What's the difference?" I asked, perturbed.

"I'm not out here killing people," he explained. "I do a lot of bad stuff, but I'm not doing that. I was just raised by the streets."

Rashad always had a way of explaining what I didn't understand.

A Blue Morning

One early morning, we met in the backyard of Aunt Cynthia's apartment.

"Hey Pretty," he greeted me with a soft smile. Leaning slightly over, he fidgeted in his pocket and held out his hand to give me something. He didn't have much, but what he always gave was meaningful. However, instead of snacks, this time, Rashad pulled out a thick wad of cash that was folded in half.

"Here," he said handing the money to me.

He's about to give me his money? I thought. *No one has ever done anything like this for me. I mean, that's what those girls in the books I read about experience, right?*

In the past, I had boys who crushed over me. Some boys wrote and passed letters to me in class, or slid folded love notes into the slots of my locker. I even got a few teddy bears of all sizes and candy on Valentine's Day, but never did a boy offer to give me money.

"I'm going to give you the world," said Rashad. It seemed there was nothing that he wouldn't do for me.

Rashad

He was rocking a D.C. haircut
No verbal skills or presentation.
Still I yearned for that thug imitation.
Only young years and happy smiles
to his daring profession and
his street class
lifestyle.

Rashad's Place

Saturdays was a day when I went to a youth program near Aunt Cynthia's new apartment where Rashad lived with his mother and baby sister.

In order to meet up with Rashad, I had to convince Momma that I was in another activity after the program ended. It was a flat out lie. I felt bad telling "a story" to Momma, but that was the only way that I could see Rashad. After getting Momma's approval, I crossed the street to where Rashad lived.

Public Housing Authority. The apartment complex was for people and families who qualified for subsidized housing and Section 8. Rashad lived right at its center. He was immune to the poverty-infested, whiskey-breathing, cigarette-chain smoking, card slapping down in the courtyard men and women who made up the neighborhood. Rashad lived right at its center. The winos. The homeless. Kids without parents playing all hours of the night without shoes. *Where are their parents?* I wondered, but this was common in the hood.

My eyes lifted to the three flights of stairs that led to Rashad's apartment. I carefully climbed each step as the scent of urine, alcohol, weed, and garbage cooked by the summer heat, stung the lining of my nose. I used my hand to block the smell, but the stench kept creeping through my fingers as a new visitor. Once I reached to the top of the stairwell that overlooked a small balcony, I knocked on the door.

"Hold on!" yelled a voice.

A woman opened the door and greeted me dryly. It was Ms. Katina, Rashad's mother. She seemed nice for the most part, but when she smiled, I wasn't sure if it was genuine or just a front. I often wondered what she said about me once I left. Nevertheless, all I knew was that she let me come over to her house to visit her son without any questions.

Although we were teenagers, Ms. Katina treated us like adults. She knew that I wasn't supposed to be over there visiting her son, but she didn't ask questions or stop me. That was one of the reasons I liked going over there so much.

"Hi, Ms. Katina," I greeted her warmly as she held her infant daughter on the side of her hip.

"Hi," she responded lukewarmly. She didn't pay me much attention. "Rashad, boy get out here. Jenesis is here."

Ms. Katina was cooking spaghetti on the stove and had the whole apartment burning up. Although I didn't know how to communicate with Ms. Katina because she never seemed to genuinely like me, I was thankful that she opened the door. Ms. Katina went back to cooking at the stove.

Rashad walked from his bedroom to the living room half-sleep rubbing his eye. He was shirtless, showing his brown chest and tight stomach. He looked like one of those small toy action figures that little boys typically have too many of scattered on the floor. He greeted me with a smile and hug before walking me to his bedroom. He closed the door, and it was just us.

Movie Night

We lie on Rashad's bed for hours, it seemed. We talked about anything and everything under the sun or moon until the Sandman snatched us up. Sometimes we would just watch our favorite movies in each other's arms. Always the Black classics from the 1990's— *Brown Sugar, Poetic Justice, The Fighting Temptations,* and *Jason's Lyric.*

Rashad's personal favorites were hood movies with all the cussing in them like *Fly By Night* and *Belly.* I rolled my eyes the first few times I watched those movies but learned to find parts in the movie that were funny to me to make the movie more entertaining.

"How do you make everything funny that's supposed to be serious?" asked Rashad.

We both laughed together while watching movies.

These black VHS tapes sat next to an old and dusty VCR under the television where our favorites movies were already out for us to easily turn on and play on rotation. No matter what we watched, our time was limited and precious, so we made sure to enjoy each other's company. He was my best friend and the only person who really understood me.

On his bed, Rashad lie on his back. His arms were pretzeled behind his head as he stared up at the ceiling. I lie on my side with one arm outstretched and lying across his chest. He rubbed the side of my head, gently, laying down the frizzy baby hair strands that escaped from my curly ponytail holder. Raising my chin, I snuck a peek at him. His chest rose and fell softly with each breath before he spoke.

"I feel like an old man in a child's body," said Rashad. He was only 17-years old, but he had lived the life of an adult. Rashad was brought up in the streets and the streets has a way of aging its victims.

How can someone so young feel so old? I wondered.

I felt sorry for Rashad. I didn't want him to struggle. I wanted to help him. To save him. To love him. My mind wandered to stories he previously told me about his early childhood and how he was taught to survive on the streets. I wanted to give him a new beginning, but all I knew how to give was love.

A Child

And I will tell you where the strength came
from.
In the pit of one woman's choked screaming
With the absence of solid tears, a thick winter
Under stretched belly branded by navel cords
united with the other.
It was on some other aged street. Began in odds
and ended with
Two feet, two arms, stalked neck and all of the
fingers. Yes,
It was where some dead persons lived at, but
you would live longer than
Any odd or even shown up on sidewalk views in
windows,
Flat, mattresses pissed out from the ones before,
boiled water peeling at the bending tub on edges.
It was where the child lost the elastic shine of
her nineteen-inch waist,
The forty-two-inch hip area and firm thighs.
Now soaked within the parallels of frost
And the odor of recycled grease that sits in the
night. Where one woman
Was brought. Sent with a new age, new
garments and told to-

Become one woman with one child all together
again, in a solid tear. Held by a candle
flickering.
Lost its scent after birth and tell you. That winter
was dreadful.
Hands swollen and cracked, picked up
Put down, shifted with opened lids, laying heavy
on dark multicolored sirens
That glistened and danced on oily, stained walls.
It's where. Stench embedded too far, between
the pull of this place and others,' cemented
walls.
From one heart beat to the next heartbeat, men
and women-those wooden dimes, the matted
scalp, the elongated stance- too much inside the
stride of their walking habits, so let's store them
in a sacred place-quiet. So, whatever's governed,
done lost their scent since birth.
And it done left much. the half smiles, the
rusting pork pots, the dry smell of roaches on a
counter top nibbling at leftovers. It's there, when
only light to use is the streets and the child is
too. Laying
Toward its single, cracking in from the
cardboard shudders, resting on child's
indentions-
The forehead. The eyes. Chest heaving up and
down. Up and down. With oldest, moving next

with the tempo. In a breath… when Momma watches from the door. The outside lamp shadows and drapes around the heavy breasts covered by a soft bed robe. She leans closer onto the walls, until the only thing found are the shapely, drawn eye sockets that are losing its density by the count. And a hollow snicker moves the child. Now, standing short legged, the most innocent Brown, tight knotted on the head and wearing nothing more than a discolored short sleeved shirt and underwear. Seen the mouth twitch for the first time, but don't really understand yet, Momma. How the tips of your fingers tug on the right side of your upper lip, numb from you becoming "a Woman." So, both stand, not understanding the other, when child moves closer in quiet stiffness that Momma left in walls like the other infants. And it's then when strength came in, waited. Losing the after-birth scent. became what some might call, man

A Family War Zone

Our families were feuding for multiple reasons but there were two main ones. First, my family wasn't too fond Rashad's family ever since Cousin Robert married Monique. They were a little rough around the edges. Actually, *ghetto*— to be quite frank.

Second, Rashad and Monique's mother, Ms. Katina stole my Grandma's purse during a family event that led the cops to Grandma's townhouse for a search warrant because her wallet and driver's license were found at a crime scene in a dope house.

Bizarre.

My family and I were upset about the whole situation; however, I didn't hold that against Rashad. That was his Momma's fault. He was innocent despite her wrongdoings. However, I would soon learn that he had his own personal struggles that had yet to be revealed.

"What do you see in me, Jenesis?" Rashad looked at me, frowning. "No one wants us to be together."

"So, what?" I replied. "I don't care. I'm not letting anybody stop us from being together."

Rashad's insecurities were getting the best of him.

"Why me when you can have anybody you want?" Rashad continued.

"I love you and I want you," I explained.

"Your family will never accept me, Jenesis."

It was a harsh and real reality that I wasn't willing to face or accept, but Rashad was right. No matter how much we loved each other, my family would not approve. Although our families were at war and didn't plan to make peace any time soon, I ignored the warning signs and red flags. Instead, Rashad and I decided to stay together no matter the battle wounds.

The Birds and the Bees

Whenever the word "sex" was spoken aloud, an emotional current of fear, shame, and paranoia circulated through every vein in my body. I felt guilty even when I wasn't doing anything remotely close to sex.

Can anyone hear or see my thoughts? I wondered. The idea and talk of "doing it" made me feel *nasty*. I knew nothing about sex besides what adults said that rang in my ears with emphasis:

"Don't *do* it!"

"You can get *pregnant*!"

"You can get *diseases* and *die*!"

All scare tactics to persuade teens from engaging in sex or better yet, "intercourse." So technical and correct. It was like a secret that everyone knew but couldn't say aloud. Just the word got people giggling, turning red, and looking away. I didn't plan on knowing the secret any time soon.

"Your body is your temple," explained Momma. "Honor and respect it. Only give your body to your husband, Jenesis."

I listened to Momma, respected my body, and honored marriage as a sacred agreement of life-long commitment. I believed marriage was the ultimate display of unconditional love and affection between two people. I was a church-going school girl who read the Bible religiously. However, while I wondered who would even want to have sex without being married, Rashad made the thought a little easier to digest.

The Right Time

There were attempts, but we both would get scared and quickly change our minds. Trial and error. We didn't travel too far from first and second base. Typical experimentation— hugging, kissing, and "clothes burning" or "dry humping." Rashad always seemed ready while I was unsure about traveling to third base. We needed a referee for this ballgame.

"I'm scared," I confessed to Rashad as we lie across his bed.

He play whined for a couple of seconds then replied, "Okay." And that was that.

We both were virgins and understood how special it was to give away our virginity— something so precious that we could never get back. The time had to be just right.

Something New

Like spring, our relationship was approaching a fresh and new season allowing us to explore new terrain. It was a feeling that would soon bud and blossom for the both of us.

We lie across Rashad's bed with a movie playing that we weren't paying any attention to. It was one of those movies that you knew by heart but use as background noise. As we watched the movie, I felt Rashad's hand slowly move from the bed to my stomach. I turned to look directly at him. The look in his eyes told me what words couldn't express.

Rashad ran his hand softly up my body to the side of my neck and brought my lips to his for a kiss, but this wasn't like our typical "make out" sessions. This was more than that. Usually, our kisses started off slow and smooth, but today, our kisses were fast and rough. Passion surged through me. For a few seconds, my body tensed as his swift movements caught me off guard. But, as I became more comfortable with this new momentum, my body softened, loosened, and leaned deeper into his.

Rashad broke away from the kiss and lifted his white T-shirt over his head revealing a smooth and defined chest. He quickly, unbuttoned and removed his jeans before tossing them to the floor. Rashad laid back against the bed in boxers with his eyes focused on me.

Confidently, I straddled him and ran my hands across his chest. This wasn't the first time that I had admired his body. However, this was the first time that I could touch. When I removed my shirt, Rashad reached behind my back and unhooked my bra leaving me fully exposed both physically and emotionally.

"You are so beautiful," he whispered. His touch sent chills through my body.

"Thank you," I whispered blushing and looking away. I didn't know what to do next, but Rashad took control and laid me back on the bed, kissing me deeply.

***

We were laid up— teenage youth. Poverty- infested room with the whole world against us. No jobs. No responsibilities. No schedules. Our limbs were entangled like tree branches. It was our first time.

Although, I planned to wait until marriage to have sex, Rashad and I justified this decision by confessing our love to each other and making secret promises to eventually get married. So, we figured, "Why wait?" Taking each other's virginity would be the ultimate profession of our love while teenagers. But afterwards, my mind raced as guilt crept in. While I trusted myself to give him my virginity, I was still worried and regretful.

Oh my God, I thought. *What would Momma think?*

Tears flooded my face like a rainstorm. I didn't realize that these April showers would soon bring May flowers. We planted a seed that would soon grow to change our lives forever.

Guilty

Before losing my virginity, I always wondered if a person felt different after having sex the first time. I imagined that it would be kind of like your birthday when you wait to feel a change— maybe wiser or more mature because you're one year older, but you really just feel the same. Nothing too significant. Just another day of the year to celebrate being who you have always been. But losing my virginity was nothing like that.

This is what it feels like to not be a virgin, I thought. I covered my face with my hands and cried.

Being a virgin was something that set me apart from my "experienced" friends and peers who practically did everything under the sun— drinking, smoking, cussing, having sex, and anything else "bad." I felt ashamed of what we, what I, had just done.

I gave away my virginity. It's over, I thought. *Now, I'm like everybody else.*

Lost in my thoughts, Rashad put his arms around me pulling me back to reality.

"I just can't believe that we aren't virgins anymore," I said. "It's just crazy. I can't believe we did it."

What will my Momma say? I thought. I knew full well what she expected of me and this was not it.

"We didn't do nothin' wrong," Rashad said confidently. He turned on his side and rested his head on his hand, while looking up at me. He was so calm as he smiled and gently kissed the back of my hand.

"Together forever," he whispered. "Promise me, forever." He linked his fingers with mine.

I felt a current surge through my body as he spoke. His words clouded by thoughts so much so, I couldn't think. All I could do was feel.

"Forever," I responded with renewed conviction.

Rashad pulled my body into his.

Secret Promises

Am I a woman now? I wasn't sure. Sex felt wrong. *Does losing my virginity make me an adult?*

I had so many questions about my new body. It was our first acquaintance.

My mind wandered.

People will look at me and know that I'm not a virgin anymore, I thought. *Especially Momma.* I couldn't imagine what she would say or do if she found out. *What if she already knows?*

Momma had what many people called "the gift of prophecy." She could *always* sense when something was about to happen.

"Something is wrong," she would say, squinting her eyes in concentration. "I can feel it."

Even without any possible clue, she would tell you exactly what was happening in the privacy of your own mind. Her gift *never* failed.

When Momma got this "feeling," before you knew it, your cover was blown. Every feeling that she felt and vision that she saw— came true. Gift of prophecy, premonition, women's intuition, discernment, psychic, supernatural abilities— call it what you want but Momma definitely had an "inside scoop."

Why did my Momma have to have "the gift?" I thought. *Just my luck.*

Moving Me On

Pregnant teenager
They were different. Different hands. Different
eyes. Different feet.
Everything was different. But what linked them
all together. You.
Said, love never came. But it burns strong all the
same.
Noticed the scarred markings under your left
eye. The moist area, inside the crease of your
neck. The dry odor stitched into the heavy black
cloth you wore. And it burned all the same. Our
adolescence. Something you never owned,
would create the burning we both needed in a
single kiss, interlocking of the palms until we
both desired more. Gave my body to you and
yours to me, on a wide mattress next to a wide
window.
"Open a little wider." And I did. Tears rolling
out of corners. Wanted
to make love, for you. But how could I? It was
taken from me.
You said, "It's okay. I love you."
I knew that you were for me. You'd unravel the
tight knots between my thighs.
The back of my left hand bent up against your
wet lips. And you are inside of me.

Hope was waiting. Inflamed and burning. How can the end live when the beginning already died? If only I would have known, then. So, I raise my eyes to meet the spirit. Where tears roll from behind. Was the child there all along?

"Gotta know which one, you say.
One died before entering.
The other died after exiting."

Lord, Jesus, please let me just keep this one.
The last one. The closest thang to her.

God says,
But he's been dead a long time.
Before, you found his lips.

No More Coins

We didn't have personal cell phones and talking on a home phone was a hit or miss. So, to solve the problem, Rashad, often called me from a family member's house. But when he was out and about, he used a payphone that required coins. Well, that was until we found a loophole.

"Try to call me right back on the number that showed up on your caller ID," said Rashad. He called me from an outside payphone by the apartment complex he lived in. "I have an extra quarter but wanna see if I can answer your call without putting money in."

"Okay," I quickly agreed. I hung up and dialed the number listed on the caller ID. The phone rang once, and Rashad answered.

Bingo. Jackpot. Cha-ching.

Now, we didn't need any quarters because we had free phone calls. We were forever discovering new ways of *finagling* things. The number to the payphone could be called and the person receiving the call wouldn't have to pay. This new discovery meant that we could talk on the phone as long as we wanted.

Rashad eventually found a payphone near his home where he posted up for most of our calls. Now, we could save our money and have a private untraceable phone conversation. It was basically a free phone and perfect solution to a couple of broke teenagers who had nothing better to do other than talk all night about God knows what.

In the pouring rain, freezing sleet, slushy snow, or fever heat, Rashad was at that loyal payphone taking free calls that lasted for hours. Talk about *dedication*.

One night, we just couldn't get off the phone.

"I feel bad that you're out there in the rain," I told Rashad, advising him to go inside. It was storming and there was a weather advisory warning for the area.

"I just wanna hear your voice," said Rashad begging me to stay on the phone.

I could tell he was freezing by the sound of his shivering voice that he tried to disguise.

"Please, go in the house," I urged. "I don't want you getting sick. It's too bad out there."

Rashad ignored my concern and spoke sweetly.

"I love you so so so so so much, Pretty." He said emphasizing the nickname that he had given me. I imagined him smiling, bouncing his knees, rubbing his hands together to create heat, and blowing into his tight fists to stay warm with only a hoodie for a coat.

"I love you too, handsome," I said, speaking clearly so that he could hear every word. "Now, go in, please, before you get sick!"

Finally, he decided to listen after much persuading. Rashad was more than my boyfriend. He was my best friend.

It's the Heart that Counts

Rashad wasn't a supermodel, but he was handsome to me.

"Here's a picture of him," I said, handing a picture of Rashad to my best friend Stephanie. In the picture, he was holding up a gang sign, wearing a bandana and a mean mug.

"Beauty and the Beast!" she said out loud, throwing her head back for a good laugh. "Girl, he is *not* cute," she looked at me with the side eye over her glasses, then back at the picture. "And, what is he throwing up? Don't tell me he's gang bangin?" She let out a quick laugh, then looked serious. "You playin', right?"

Dang, she's judging! I thought. *I can't tell this girl nothin'!*

Ignoring her reaction, I pointed to the picture, trying to defend him.

"Look at his cute eyes," I said. "I love those sad-puppy dog eyes."

Stephanie stared at me unimpressed. "But do you see everything else in the picture? Girl, he's throwin' up a gang sign!"

"I know," I said, sighing and looking away.

Can this girl be happy for me? I thought. Embarrassed, I quickly grabbed the picture from her hands.

Stephanie gave me that, *I know you ain't snatchin' stuff,* look. But I didn't care that she had an attitude. I did too. I couldn't help feeling disappointed because I thought her reaction would have been different.

We don't have no support, I thought.

"He said he's gonna stop because I don't want him doing that," I explained, trying to persuade Stephanie to think differently about him, but it didn't work. Instead, she pursed her lips, rolled her eyes, and looked off in the distance. She was acting like a Momma. Not like my best friend. I guess, I needed it though. Instead of meeting her with the same attitude, I tried to lighten the mood.

"It's what's in the heart that counts," I said, holding up a heart shape with my hands while making a pout face, trying to be funny.

We both laughed. My plan worked. The mood was lightened. But who was I fooling? Stephanie still didn't like Rashad. She wouldn't be the first or last either. Now, I had to make sure I didn't tell her too much about the relationship.

Part FOUR

The Peace Treaty

A Homeless City

With family struggles, Rashad was in and out of his Momma's house, crashing on his family members couches, and living homeless on the streets. He just couldn't catch a break. I felt bad knowing that he was outside all hours of the night, sleeping at the park, and anywhere else he could temporarily lay his head.

No one deserves to live that way. Especially no one in my life, I thought.

So, thinking with my emotions rather than with logic, I came up with an idea.

"You can stay at my house for a little while until you find another place to stay," I said. "You don't need to be sleeping outside. It's too dangerous."

Although hesitant and fearful of the outcome, after a little persuading, Rashad agreed to the plan.

"Here, take this," I said, placing a spare house key in Rashad's hand. "Don't let anyone find out. Promise me."

"I promise baby," professed Rashad. Thank you so much."

Young Love

It was the first week of my 11th grade year. Rashad had been secretly staying at our house for days now without anyone knowing and the last thing we needed was to be outed which was definitely possible especially with a nosy little brother like mine.

See, for the past three days, Christopher admitted to hearing noises and witnessing shadows moving under my bedroom door. He even brought our two furry white Bichon Frise puppies in on it.

We stood in the hallway as Christopher shared his observations.

"I keep hearing something in there and the dogs keep running to the door and smelling under it," he said with a frightened look on his face.

Like any other time, Momma took his noticing's with a grain of salt. Christopher loved scary movies. They always left him with a sixth sense, afraid of the dark, and wondering if there were ghosts in the house.

"Momma, I think Jenesis' room is possessed," explained Christopher. "There's something in there."

"There's nothing in there," Momma said. She was used to Christopher's bizarre accusations.

As he spoke, I stared him down, hoping he'd stop talking, but my telekinesis-mind-reading powers didn't work like I always wanted it to.

"There's nothing in there," I explained, agreeing with Momma.

But my little brother wouldn't stop talking.

"Yes, it is!" he insisted. "I hear it!"

Momma shook it off as an effect of watching too many scary movies. However, little did she know, he was really onto something, but it wasn't a ghost. It was Rashad.

A Birthday Surprise

August 25th. Before we left the house for Momma to drop me and Christopher off at our respective schools, I reminded Rashad to follow my instructions carefully. I was very clear.

"Do not make any noise," I said. "Remember not to leave the room until you hear my Momma close and lock the door."

Rashad agreed.

The plan was simple enough, but even a tiny glitch in the system could cause the whole thing to come crashing down, which was why it was so important for him to follow directions. However, Rashad chose to divert from the plan.

After he heard my Momma leave the house, he unlocked the bedroom door, grabbed a plate of food from the kitchen, and returned to my room to watch the family comedy— *Meet the Parents*— just the right movie for the occasion.

Rashad had gotten sloppy with the plan. He wasn't being watchful and cautious anymore. Instead, he got comfortable with the routine and that's when all hell broke loose. See, although Momma had left to drop me and Christopher off at school, he didn't realize it, but she had returned home and invited her twin sisters over to celebrate their birthday. They were in the basement salon talking and watching an all-time family favorite— a Tyler Perry *Madea* movie. However, as they watched the movie, Momma's keen sense of hearing kicked in when she heard rustling upstairs.

"Y'all hear that?" Momma's eyes searched the ceiling.

"No," replied Cynthia who looked at her sister puzzled. "What are you talking about? I don't hear anything."

"I don't either," replied Tasha.

"I just heard something fall upstairs," Momma said, looking back up at the ceiling.

"It's probably just the pipes," explained Cynthia. She always thought her sister was a little paranoid.

But Momma wasn't giving up that easily. She continued to look at the ceiling. See, Momma knew exactly where noises came from based on where she was in the house. Her senses were always on point.

"No, I know I hear something," said Momma. "It's coming from Jenesis' room."

Cynthia and Tasha looked at each other confused. They still didn't hear anything, but they knew their sister had a strong sense of discernment. So, when Momma heard the noise coming from my room, all three of them went upstairs to "check it out." Tasha grabbed a butcher knife from the kitchen. Cynthia grabbed my color guard flag from the living room closet. And Momma grabbed all she needed— her fists that were straight out of Detroit. All three of them stood outside of my bedroom door.

By that time, Rashad had already heard footsteps coming up the basement stairs and quickly found a hiding place.

Standing at the locked bedroom door with weapons drawn, Momma picked the lock and opened the door. Their eyes thoroughly searched and inspected the room— a plate of half-eaten leftover food sat in the middle of the floor and a movie was playing. They walked over to both bedroom closets. Aunt Cynthia opened one of the closets and jabbed through the clothes with the flag pole.

"Nothing in there," said Cynthia.

They walked over to the final closet and slid back one of the doors. Clothes were bunched on the shelves, hanging up, and a pile of clothes lie stacked on the floor. Cynthia went in again, jabbing through the closet and beating up the clothes with the flag pole.

"Well if there's anyone in there, then they got beat the hell out of," said Cynthia.

They all laughed while standing at the closet until they saw one of the hangers suddenly move and the pile of clothes on the floor, shake.

"Oh shit!" yelled Tasha. "Someone's really in there!"

They were ready for whatever was about to go down. Whoever was in there was about to get laid out. With weapons drawn, they prepared to defend themselves. Momma grabbed the side of the closet door to slide it back, until she heard a voice coming from inside.

"Wait!" yelled the voice. "It's Rashad!"

"What the hell?!" yelled Momma.

She quickly slid back the closet door and there stood Rashad— half-braided, bare-chested with jeans, and apologizing. The room grew smaller as Momma's body grew twice her size and transformed into something similar to the Incredible Hulk with a deep voice.

"Get out of my house!" yelled Momma who picked up an object to hit Rashad.

Cynthia and Tasha slowly backed up against the wall, withdrawing their weapons. Their sister pretty much had it covered.

Lifting up from getting hit, Rashad stood upright and balled his fists like he was about to do something. He was bucking up to the wrong Momma. She was not to be tested.

"What you gon' do?" asked Momma. Rashad had no other choice but to loosen his fists. He knew not to swing. Instead, he attempted to grab his keys on the table, but Momma snatched the keys before he could.

"These are not your keys! These are mine— now, get out my house!"

Putting on his shirt, Rashad grabbed his shoes as fast as he could, but Momma had already called the police and they were on their way. Frantically, Rashad rushed towards the bedroom door to leave, but Momma had another escape route in mind.

"No, not my door," ordered Momma. "Out the window. Get out the way you came in!"

Climbing out the window, Rashad ran down the street. By the time the police arrived, he was already long gone.

Tasha stared blankly into space and shook her head in disbelief.

"How long has he been here?" she asked, as her voice trailed off.

"I don't know," said Momma, but I'm asking Jenesis as soon as I pick her up."

Caught

I sat on the front steps of my high school campus awaiting Momma to pick me up like she always did, until my phone rang with an unknown number. When I answered the phone, I wasn't ready for what was to come.

"We're caught!" said Rashad. He sounded out of breath.

"What?" I panicked. "You're kidding!" All sorts of thoughts flooded my mind. "What happened?" I asked covering my face with my hands.

"They found me in the closet and as soon as I got out of there, I called you," explained Rashad.

"Where are you?"

"At a payphone down the street from your house."

This can't be happening, I thought.

As I plotted our escape, my mind was blurry. I couldn't hear my thoughts. I was typically good at coming up with a plan, but today, I was drawing a blank. That was until one of our secret hideout places came to mind— the university library across the street from my school.

"Meet me in the library on campus," I directed.

"Okay," said Rashad. "I'm on my way."

I sped-walked to the library, all the while looking around to make sure I didn't see Momma's car. I anticipated a flood of incoming calls, warning me of Momma's wrath that was forthcoming, but no one called.

I couldn't imagine what Momma was thinking about me after finding Rashad in the house. I could feel my racing heartbeat in my temples. My head was throbbing from all the worry and I couldn't think straight. All I could do was feel. I feared for what I knew was to come when I finally got that call and answered. We did a lot of risky things, but this definitely took the cake.

"If anyone calls, I'm not answering my phone," I told Rashad. "And I'm definitely not going back home to face Momma any time soon."

Our Secret Hideout

After hiding out in the library and being M.I.A. for a few hours, Momma started calling my cell phone. The library was closing for the day, which meant I would have to face Momma sooner than I wanted to. Taking a deep breath, I answered the phone, but Momma sounded normal like nothing was wrong. She didn't mention anything.

This is strange, I thought after the phone call.

Momma was on her way to pick me up and I needed to head back soon, so Rashad and I parted ways at the library and I walked back to the front of my school. But just like I thought, when Momma picked me up, and I got into the car, she had something to share.

"How are you doing today?" asked Momma, nonchalantly while driving. But before I could answer, she continued. "Guess what? Rashad was at the house today."

I was shocked and couldn't read her expression. I just sat there staring out the window into traffic like a deer in headlights. I didn't know what to do. I was a nervous wreck, awaiting Momma's fury that was ready to explode. She was a quiet storm ready to pour down on me. I wasn't prepared for the natural disaster that was to come.

"Let me out!" I urged. My mind went wild. I did not want to see how much this storm could tear me apart.

"Why?" asked Momma, looking perplexed. "So, you can go look for Rashad?" She was still speaking in that crazy-calm voice.

My thoughts were scrambled, and my brain was foggy. I had no words. I felt so guilty and ashamed for what I had done. My eyes filled with tears before I spoke.

"I never should have let him in," I said shaking my head in a daze. "I'm sorry, Momma."

Momma was angry and disappointed in me, but she forgave me. However, it would take time for her to trust me again.

While apologetic, I was young, in love, and willing to go the distance for Rashad, even if it meant breaking Momma's trust that I was trying to rebuild. But soon, I wouldn't be just breaking Momma's trust. I would be breaking Momma's heart, and that hurt the worst.

The Peace Treaty

Rashad was my first love. We spoke our truth on his bed near an open window. Lying and hugging each other as the cool summer breeze calmed the evening sun.

"I'm gonna protect you," he said staring up at the ceiling. "Just never leave me."

"Okay," I said, looking up at him and squeezing him tighter.

"I'm gonna give you the world. I promise."

I believed him as the sound of city noise and people talking outside flowed through the bedroom.

Going nowhere, but love

The clouds hover me over...
Makes my path,
Water trails
Aqua waterfalls and butterfly kisses...
With my legs, I ran
tripping over the rocks and logs that laid ahead
of me... I dared not stop.
My hair blew in spite of the pain
With the wind, I blew your secrets
and... I touched your rainfall tears
They drowned your cries
When I touched your features,
Holding them in my palm.
I never knew I could
love someone the way
I loved you.
How could we
Combine to create such a dream
holding love songs
and private poems
I never knew,
me and you...
could be such a beautiful dream
me and you...

A Pinky Promise

I don't know who said it first, but we both agreed that it was the only way that we would be connected forever. We figured that if we had a baby, our families would have no other choice, but to accept us. So, we made a decision, interlocked our pinkies, and a kiss sealed the promise to make our peace treaty.

Symptoms

It was late October and football season was ramping up in our hometown. While everyone looked forward to Friday night football games, I was eager for our marching band performances. It was my senior year in color guard and I finally had a solo to show my skills center stage at the game.

While some band members packed up the school bus to travel across town to the stadium, others got dressed in the restrooms. I went into the girl's restroom to change into my costume.

Girls in the band were everywhere, inside and outside of the stalls, changing their clothes in front of each other. I always liked my privacy, so I went into an empty stall to change my clothes, but when I put on my sequined top, it felt tighter than usual.

Why is my top so tight? I wondered.

Although I had been bloated for the last couple of days, I didn't think more into it because my body always looked and felt the same. Same flat stomach. Same size legs. Same look no matter how many bags of chips and packages of candy I ate, but tonight was different. However, I quickly shrugged off the strange feeling— my mind had to be ready for the debut of my solo. Nothing was going to distract me. Plus, Rashad was going to be there watching me in the stands. Just thinking of him made a smile spread across my face— no matter how tight and uncomfortable my costume was.

***

A few weeks after my stellar color guard solo, I noticed other changes in my body.

One evening, Momma cooked me and my brother's favorite— broccoli and cheddar soup. The first bite was delicious, but as soon as I took the second bite, I felt the urge to vomit. My stomach muscles contracted. I became dizzy and the room got real hot. Covering my mouth, I ran as fast as I could into the bathroom farthest from the kitchen in Momma's bedroom.

Sitting on my knees and hugging the toilet in front of me, every bit of soup I had just ate, poured out of me. My eyes were watery as the stomach acid burned my throat.

What's going on? I wondered. *I never get sick.*

And that's when, after catching my breath and blinking away tears, I looked up at the pink tiled bathroom wall, and thought for the first time— *am I pregnant?*

Results

The city bus ride was short, but it felt longer because of all the thoughts that swarmed in my head as I headed to the clinic. To calm my nerves, I read a chapter in *The Autobiography of Malcolm X* to pass time. That was the latest book that I was reading— an Alex Haley classic— and was sure to distract me from my racing thoughts.

There were only two other people on the bus. And with my face buried in my book, it was clear that I didn't want to talk, but that didn't stop a young man who was sitting across from me from speaking.

"I'm on my way to a McDonald's interview," he said proudly.

"Mmhmm," I responded, briefly lifting my eyes and eyebrows to acknowledge him before returning to my book.

"Do you have a job?" he continued.

In my mind, my head dropped backwards, and my eyes rolled into the back of my head at the thought of having to talk to this guy. I did not feel like talking.

Before I could think of something to tell him, thankfully, the bus slowed down at my stop, allowing me to quickly escape.

Saved by the bus! I thought.

Courteously, I gave him a polite closed-mouth smile and quick response before making my way off the bus that stopped directly in front of the building that I was headed into. I didn't know the guy or owe him an explanation but didn't want to be rude.

"I have an interview to become an intern here," I lied.

"Good luck!" he yelled back. But I was already off the bus, walking toward the building.

After I was buzzed in, I entered the clinic and looked around. The answer to every question that anyone could possibly have about sex, pregnancy, and sexually transmitted diseases were posted on the walls and in pamphlets that sat on the waiting room tables.

Looking around, there were a few other girls waiting to be seen. I signed my name on the clipboard and waited to be called back. A shiver crept up the back of my neck as nervousness took hold. Trying to shake the anxious feeling, I went into my book bag to finish reading the chapter that I had started on the bus. While it helped a little, I couldn't ignore the sudden queasiness that came with overthinking and analyzing how I ended up in that very chair.

Finally, the nurse called my name.

"Hi sweetie," she said. The nurse had short, dark brown hair and was wearing a long white lab coat. "The restroom is right here." She held a clear, labeled container with a top on it. "Pee in this cup, and afterwards, place it in the small metal box. We will collect your urine sample from there." Her words were quick and straight to the point. She continued, "When you're finished, wait in this room," she pointed to a room nearby.

The restroom was cold and sterile. Following the nurse's directions, I placed my sample inside the metal box, washed my hands, and went into the patient room. It was a regular hospital room with the bare minimum of a bed, stool, sink area, and a counter with all types of equipment. But what caught my attention the most were the posters that followed me from the waiting area to the hospital room. There wasn't a space on the wall without a poster.

They definitely want you to learn a lesson while you're here, I thought.

Posters with sad-looking pregnant teenagers in baggy clothes and national statistics about STDs covered the walls. The teenagers in the posters seemed to stare down at me from the white walls. I recognized the shame in their eyes as I felt the same way— alone, until the nurse walked in. It felt like it had been an eternity, but it really had only been about fifteen minutes. I was relieved to see her, but still nervous and afraid. Although, I wanted to be pregnant as the idea of having a baby was something I wanted, I was still uncertain about a few things.

"Yes. You are pregnant," said the nurse. Her face was sullen as she spoke. "Now, what are you gonna do?"

I was not only shocked by the news, but by her bedside manners that took me aback. Her words echoed in my mind as I looked around the hospital room and searched for a response in silence. The teenagers from the posters who once looked depressed, now looked like they were smiling at me— an insidious smile that signaled a sense of *we knew all along you were pregnant*. Now, the poster children for teen pregnancy had someone to share their statistics with. It wouldn't be long before I joined them on the wall of shame.

While I was in disbelief of the news, I was also excited that I actually was pregnant— a plan between Rashad and I that actually worked. I was hopeful in how we said we would move forward with having our baby. Being a mother, wife, college student, and writer were always an aspiration of mine. I planned to accomplish all of my goals.

So, with all that in mind, I had no problem telling the nurse, "It's a little sooner than I expected, but I'm going to have this baby like I planned with my boyfriend."

Telling Aunt Cynthia

Heading back toward the lobby, all I could think of was, *how am I going to tell Momma?* I had to tell someone. I couldn't keep it to myself.

I hadn't thought it all through yet, but Aunt Cynthia quickly came to mind. We were seven years apart, but me and Cynthia were close. She knew exactly what it felt like to be a pregnant teenager because she had experienced it herself. The only difference was she didn't have someone to confide in when she was pregnant.

"Can I use your phone to make a call?" I asked the receptionist at the front desk.

"Sure, you can," she responded.

I called Aunt Cynthia and after a couple of rings, she was on the phone.

"Hey, it's me, Jenesis," I said.

"Hey!" she greeted.

"I have to tell you something."

"Okay," she responded with a hint of concern and hesitation in her voice.

I didn't know how to say it and I didn't know how she would react to the news, but I just let it roll from my tongue the best way I could.

"I'm pregnant."

There was a brief pause before she spoke.

"Where are you?" asked Aunt Cynthia.

"The Family Health Center," I replied.

And just like that, she was on her way to get me.

***

"You need a prenatal appointment," stressed Aunt Cynthia as she drove me to her house.

Although I was apprehensive to be pregnant and that Momma would find out, Aunt Cynthia didn't focus on that. Her biggest concern was making sure that both the baby and I were healthy. She was not only a concerned aunt, but a student in nursing school who also worked at a hospital. Her talk helped calm my nerves about the whole situation.

"I don't know how or when to tell my Momma," I said, dazed while staring out the window. "What should I do?"

Aunt Cynthia could see the fear in me. At one time, she had the same look on her face, but she made sure to put the responsibility back on me when she said, "It isn't for me to tell."

Aunt Cynthia explained the importance of taking a daily multivitamin with folic acid and scheduling my first doctor's appointment. She was my first ally. I was truly thankful for her.

On the Sidewalk

I have a baby growing inside of me, I thought. It just didn't feel real.

Even though we planned to get pregnant, I still didn't know how to tell Rashad. *Wanting* to be a parent was one thing. Actually, *being* a parent was a whole different story. So, I was naturally worried and nervous to reveal the news. I didn't know how he would respond.

I grabbed my phone to call Rashad but when he picked up, I quickly realized this was the type of news that you talk about in person and not over the phone.

"I have something important to tell you," I said. "I'm on my way over there now."

Within the hour, we stood facing each other on the sidewalk between the apartment complex and bus station under the blue evening sky and streetlights. Every emotion in me settled heavy and deep in my gut. I could feel the gravity of its pull weighing on me. I didn't know how to tell Rashad that he was going to be a Daddy. All I knew was that this is what we wanted, planned, and finally got. Finally, the words came out of my mouth in a voice that wasn't my own.

"I'm pregnant," I told Rashad. "And, I don't know what to do."

Rashad heard the doubt in my voice and automatically jumped to the conclusion that I didn't want the baby.

"I know you're not thinking about getting an abortion," said Rashad angrily and accusingly. "That's not gon' happen."

"Of course not," I replied offended that he would make such an assumption. "I'm happy, I'm just scared. I wasn't sure of how you would respond."

Rashad had that distant look in his eye like he sometimes got. It was always hard to read his emotions, but anger always seemed to stand out the most. I could tell he was in a mood, so I was ready to leave and go home. However, as I tried to leave, he grabbed me tightly by my arm and wouldn't let me leave.

"Rashad, I have to leave," I told him, taken aback by his aggressiveness. But he wasn't hearing me. Unbeknownst to me, this would soon become a pattern of Rashad's violent behavior.

Since u love me so.

Since u loved me
so
would u ever let me
go
if I had your baby?

After you've touched my healing
would u ever care about
my feeling
if I had your baby

So
since u love me so
I wont let u go
because your promise was
to love & keep this
baby.

A Secret Pregnancy

It was the beginning of Autumn when I visited the emergency room for my first ultrasound.

Growing up, I didn't have health insurance, so unaware of other options, the emergency room was the only other place that I could think to go— that's where I heard my baby's heart beat for the first time. I also learned how far along I was— three months. The ultrasound made everything seem more real, but I was scared to death for how Momma would react to the news.

As a result of this fear, instead of telling her right off the jump and being honest, I hid my pregnancy until I started "showing." I knew I would have to eventually tell her no matter how afraid I was. I just wasn't sure when I would.

***

After two months, I finally found the courage to tell Momma. One evening, I decided to break the news. Momma and I were in the kitchen and I felt guilty to be pregnant and so far along without her knowing. However, it was time to tell the truth, to reveal the secret that I had been hiding with sweatshirts and baggy pants.

"I need to tell you something, Momma," I said, breaking the silence as she cooked.

Christopher was there, and I knew that I couldn't tell Momma in front of him.

Her face changed immediately as she turned off the stove and motioned me down the hall into her bedroom.

My mother always spoke against pregnant teenagers and now her only daughter and oldest child was just that. Momma had such high hopes and dreams for me. I could only imagine her reaction after I revealed the truth.

Sitting at the edge of her bed, I couldn't hold it in any longer.

"Momma, I'm pregnant," I confessed.

In that moment, I felt like a failure. Whether she accepted this pregnancy or not, I knew that it would still be heartbreaking news. I just wanted her to be happy for me— for us.

"I already knew," said Momma, sighing.

Momma's discernment never failed. I couldn't believe she knew all along. I didn't know how to feel.

"I was waiting for you to tell me," she said.

Looking at Momma, all I could do was cry. I felt so regretful.

"I'm so sorry, Momma," I said. "I didn't want to disappoint you."

She wrapped her arms around me. "It's going to be alright," she said. "I love you."

Determined to Succeed

After Momma knew that I was pregnant, and Rashad was the father, the lectures started. Everyone talked at us— my Momma, uncles, aunt's boyfriends, father figures from church, and teachers— Lord knows everybody tried to give us some kind of unwanted advice.

It was no surprise that Rashad always got "the third degree" from everybody who thought he wasn't the best choice for me to have a child with since he was a middle school dropout and juvenile delinquent.

Any time Rashad did or said something inappropriate or questionable, Momma was always quick to remind him, "We don't need you. We can raise the baby without you."

Momma was always the protective type, but now that I was pregnant, she was stricter than ever before. School was another place where adults shared their opinion about my pregnancy.

"You can finish at a high school that helps teen mothers get their diploma while learning about their unborn child," explained one of my teachers.

I appreciated the fact that the school was an option, but no matter what they said and how they dressed it up, I was not leaving my high school to go there. Period. Point-blank. End of the story.

I was already a senior in my last semester of school and about to graduate. Plus, I was taking a "baby class" that taught me everything I needed to know about starting a family. I didn't need to go to a different school and I made that *very* clear to my teachers by showing them that a teenager who was pregnant could still maintain a high GPA, and remain committed to school clubs, after school programs, and community-based youth programs that would grant me a full scholarship to college.

Pregnancy didn't hinder me from accomplishing my goals. I was unstoppable. I wasn't going to let anyone discourage me from achieving any of my dreams. I started strong. I was going to finish strong. I was in it to win it—pregnant or not.

Routine Doctor Visits

Although I believed in myself, as I got further along in the pregnancy, I realized that many others didn't. This cognizance was mostly visible during routine doctor appointments.

After several visits, we quickly noticed that many of the nurses and doctors in the office didn't treat us as nicely and fairly in comparison to other pregnant women who were either White, married, or had top-of-the-line health insurance. I was a Black, unmarried, pregnant teenager with government-funded health insurance.

Whether I was standing in the line to apply for and accept federal assistance for low-income pregnant women, or waiting to be seen by the baby doctor, I could feel the stares of the white office staff who checked me in with stony faces that lacked any sign of compassion. Their prejudiced stares said everything their lips wouldn't. It was subliminal and between the lines of their monotone voices and scripted answers as they looked down at my belly with judgement. I was just another Black pregnant teen in their eyes and locked in their minds as one of *those* kinds of girls. I was nothing to them.

It was evident by the way they treated us, that the healthcare industry was yet another unjust system. It was a painful reality to face. If only I could tell them that I was an honor roll student who planned the pregnancy with my boyfriend at the time, but they wouldn't care even if I bothered. I wanted to scream at the top of my lungs to anyone who would listen to my truth. However, in reality, even though it was a planned pregnancy, I knew deep down inside, it wasn't the best decision. It was just the only option that Rashad and I could think of to keep us together.

Baby Names

We were five months along and it was time for the big gender reveal during the ultrasound.

"It's a girl!" announced the nurse. The news was a pleasant surprise.

Prior to knowing the baby's gender, I had already done research on hundreds of baby names and compiled my list of favorites and their meanings. I finally settled on one.

"I have a name that I really like for the baby," I shared with my closest friends in the school cafeteria.

Sitting around the wooden table, we talked about the naming process and my future as a new mom. I planned to give her a good life and it needed to start with the pregnancy.

The food that one consumes and the words that one speaks has the power to build and heal. My goal was to nurture and develop a healthy and brilliant child, and I did.

Super conscious about the food that me and the baby ate, my diet consisted of majority fruit and vegetable smoothies, turkey sandwiches, salads, and grilled chicken. And when it came to words, choosing a name that made a statement was paramount.

"Her name is Summer," I publicized to my friends.

I wanted to name my daughter for the season she was conceived in. However, after much persuading from Momma about the name, another one was chosen— Nadia which meant Hope. But while I fell in love with it, Rashad wasn't sold. He wanted to have a more active role in the pregnancy and exercise his voice as a soon-to-be-father. So, it wasn't a surprise when he said that he wanted to be a part of the baby naming process. I was glad that he was taking the necessary steps to be involved in the plans for our baby's life and future.

"Since you and your Momma picked out the first name, I wanna pick out the middle name," said Rashad, grinning with excitement.

"What name are you thinking about," I asked curiously.

Lord knows, Rashad was known to sometimes come up with some *off the wall* stuff that had me wondering what he was thinking, but I gave him the benefit of the doubt and listened.

"I like the name, Michelle," he said, looking at me and awaiting my reaction.

It wasn't my first choice, but I thought the name was cute and loved the fact that he wanted to be involved. However, I fell in love with the name after I did a search for its meaning and agreed to it. Nadia means "Hope." Michelle means "With God." Our daughter's name would mean "Hope with God"— the perfect name for the perfect baby.

Metamorphosis

Although Rashad promised that he would get out of the drug game, he continued to "make moves" in the streets. He didn't stop selling drugs like I wanted, but he slowed down his street hustle and got a legitimate job.

With his new income, he took on more financial responsibility as a father and partner for our growing family. However, while Rashad was on a financial "come up," he was still battling with demons.

We were getting into more arguments that mostly centered around cheating accusations against me that were based on his personal insecurities. I always reassured him of my love and that I wasn't going anywhere, but he never believed me. His demons were most visible during celebratory times, behind closed doors, and in the public eye.

There was a change in Rashad. He was becoming controlling, aggressive, and violent. I didn't know what to make of it, but I hoped things would get better. Only time would tell.

Restroom Confessions

One argument in particular was a turning point in how I was feeling as an eight-month pregnant mother who was unsure of Rashad's permanency in me and the baby's life. He emotional state was starting to get out of hand and I didn't have time to focus on just his problems. I had my own struggles and needed to focus my attention on the baby.

As I sat behind the desk in my senior English class, I couldn't stop thinking about the argument, so I asked to be excused to the restroom. Walking down that long, empty and narrow hallway, I felt the heaviness of my belly as my daughters' hands and elbows pressed against my skin from the womb. When I entered the restroom, I was met by my reflection in the wide and lengthy mirror. I rested my right hand on the top of my belly and my left hand under its curve. I was carrying a lot— dealing with being pregnant, my family hating Rashad, relationship issues, school, and my future. Overwhelmed, I stared at my reflection in the mirror and thought about my unborn child.

"I guess it's just gonna be you and me," I said while rubbing my swollen belly.

I wasn't sure how long I would keep reaffirming Rashad that I was loyal. I imagined the future, but it was too far away, and I couldn't see it clearly.

A Bag of Bibs

Throughout the nine months of pregnancy, we were blessed to have three baby showers to celebrate Nadia's arrival. Momma, Rashad's co-workers, and my teachers and friends at school all had planned individual showers.

Everyone was so excited about this child who would soon arrive. Even Christopher saved his money and bought his first niece two dresses. It was the first time that he had ever bought a "baby outfit." He couldn't wait to see her with it on.

When we finally got all the gifts home, we had everything that expecting parents could ever want and need— diapers, wipes, bottles, breast pump, crib, car seat, a diaper disposal, tons of clothes, shoes, hair ribbons, and a large bag filled with nothing but bibs. I had never seen so many bibs in my life.

"I'm thankful, but how many times is the baby gonna spit up?" I asked.

We all laughed while sorting through cards and storing away gifts in my bedroom that doubled as a nursery. We were only a few weeks away from my last doctor's appointment and we could hardly wait.

Family Dinner

May 17th. It was the day before my senior trip and final prenatal appointment. To celebrate, Momma fried fish for dinner and invited Rashad over for the first time.

Although, it took some time, Momma was finally coming around to accept Rashad and our relationship. I guess she was coming to terms with the fact that Rashad was going to be in our lives because of the baby, despite how she personally felt about him.

Dinner was prepared, and the heavy aroma of crispy fried cod and tilapia fish filled the whole house. At the table, we talked about our expectations for my final pregnancy appointment, during which, I anticipated finding out if I could be induced to give birth one week prior to my due date.

Over the past week, we packed an overnight red luggage bag and filled the baby's diaper bag with everything we could possibly need. We were prepared and ready for labor and delivery.

As we ate dinner, Rashad had an idea.

"Let's take a walk around the block," he whispered in my ear. He wanted some alone time.

Although hesitant and worried, I convinced Momma to let us go.

"We're just gonna walk around the block," I said. "We'll be right back."

Momma agreed and watched from the door to make sure all was well. Walking through the neighborhood hand-in-hand, we stopped in an alley where Rashad spoke with passion.

"I can't believe you're gonna have my baby," said Rashad.

Touching my round belly, he smiled, wrapped his arms around me, lifted me in the air, and kissed me deeply. We were going to have the family that we always wanted. I had never seen him so happy.

Full Moon

When dinner was over, Rashad went home, Momma cleaned the kitchen, Christopher fell asleep across the couch, and I lie in bed, unable to sleep as my thoughts about the next day's appointment kept me awake.

Rubbing my swollen belly, I looked out the window at a full moon. It shone brightly through the thin white curtains, casting strange shadows across my stomach. Watching the moon, my eyes grew heavy and I fell into a deep sleep.

Mother's Intuition

May 18th. I felt a weight in my stomach that I hadn't felt before.

That morning, after going into the bathroom and noticing "spotting," I told Momma and she immediately called the doctor's office.

To make sure everything was okay, Momma spoke with the on-call nurse to schedule an ultrasound. The woman on the phone was the same nurse from my routine appointments who we previously had problems with. The nurse spoke, lacking any sign of compassion or empathy as usual.

"Well, she has been coming here a lot lately and has an appointment scheduled for later this evening," replied the nurse. "Maybe you all should just wait to come in."

Momma's tone became blunt as she said, "She needs to be seen this morning and we just want to make sure the baby is fine."

"Put her on speakerphone," I whispered, annoyed by the nurse. "I wanna hear."

I was tired of this woman and how she always disregarded me and my baby. She didn't seem to have a compassionate bone in her body. I was proved right when the nurse said that famous line that all expecting mothers hate to hear when they're worried about their unborn child, "She needs to just try to get some rest."

"Try to get some rest?" I repeated in my regular voice, stunned by her careless response to an emergency.

I was pissed, and Momma was too.

"Well, my daughter is not feeling well, and we are concerned about the baby," explained Momma. "She saw blood when she went to the bathroom and that's why we're worried— it's not normal for a pregnant woman to be bleeding like that. She needs to have an ultrasound."

"Does she have her blue and pink belts?"

"We can't find them," my mother explained. She was becoming angry.

Due to past visits to the hospital, we were told by hospital staff that in order to have an ultrasound, a specific type of belts was needed for the monitor. However, we couldn't find those belts anywhere and thought it would be likely that they could be easily replenished by the hospital. Needless to say, we didn't expect the nurse's response.

"I can't do the ultrasound without those belts," said the nurse.

Momma, trying her best to hold her cool, snapped back, "So, you're telling me that you can't give an emergency ultrasound without those two belts?"

I couldn't take it anymore.

"Just forget it," I said, completely fed up. "Just hang up the phone."

Walking back into my room, I couldn't believe that they would deny a pregnant woman an emergency ultrasound because of some "belts" that they probably had a whole stock of in the hospital. I was livid.

This isn't fair, I thought walking back into the bathroom to conduct another self-examination. *This isn't right.* I checked to see if the bleeding had stopped and hoped for a different outcome, but immediately saw blood again.

Fearful, I told Momma and she made a few other phone calls to the doctor's office but they all said the same thing— like a broken record, "We can't do the ultrasound without those belts."

Without any further medical instruction, Momma advised me to stay home, but I had missed so many days already and it was the day of the senior trip.

If I'm not going to the doctor, then I'm going to school, I decided. I was stressed and needed to think positively.

"I'm just gonna go to school since it's the trip today," I told Momma.

She tried to persuade me to stay home, but I wouldn't listen. I got dressed and we headed to my school.

Senior Trip

After an afternoon of sightseeing, we boarded a large dinner boat which sailed the Ohio River. We had everything— food, music, dancing, and friends. It would be a trip to remember.

I was nine months pregnant, about to become a mother, graduate from high school, and attend college on a full scholarship. Plus, I had the support and encouragement of my family and friends around me. I was glad that I went to school. I needed some cheering up.

This was also the day of my final doctor's appointment. With my due date on my graduation day, my worst fear was my water breaking while receiving my diploma on stage. I imagined walking wide legged with my arms way out to my sides, wobbling with a big pregnant belly, and walking off the stage and down the steps to get to the hospital— a total nightmare.

"I don't want to go into labor walking across the stage to get my diploma," I explained a few months prior.

We all laughed, and the doctor agreed to see about inducing me with an epidural to deliver the baby one-week earlier than my due date. I was over the moon.

All of the seniors were dispersed throughout the boat, while my friends and I sat and talked at a dinner table catching up on all the gossip and drama that I had missed when suddenly the heaviness in my stomach returned— that sick and empty feeling.

My friend Sherise noticed the concerned expression on my face as I touched my stomach, pressing gently on each side.

"What's wrong?" she asked.

"The baby's not moving," I replied, confused with my hands placed on my belly. "Usually, when I eat, she moves."

"She's probably asleep," she replied, reassuring me that everything was fine.

"Yeah, maybe so," I said, but deep down, I could feel something was wrong as my thoughts went back to what I saw in the bathroom and the conversation with the nurse earlier that morning.

For the rest of the trip, I couldn't concentrate. I was ready for my doctor's appointment. As soon as the trip was over, Momma picked me up and we headed to the doctor's office.

Part FIVE

Love & Loss

Silence

I remember it like it was yesterday. We arrived at the hospital with the red luggage bag, prepared for labor and delivery at the hospital. We packed that bag like I was going on vacation. It had everything we could possibly need. We had all kinds of stuff in the bag including a brand new silky pink robe for me to wear while holding my newborn baby.

Momma picked me up from school and called Rashad to let him know that we were headed to the hospital. Since Rashad didn't have a driver's license or own a vehicle, he caught a taxi and met us at the doctor's office. Thankfully, he was used to my hunger pains and arrived with food in tow.

After the nurse walked us back to a small room filled with equipment typical of a doctor's office where we waited for the doctor Rashad opened the food bag in his hand and handed me and Momma an apple pie.

"Aww," said Momma smiling. "Thank you, Rashad."

"You're welcome," he said.

It felt good to see them getting along and smiling. It was the first time Rashad bought Momma something. I could see Momma was starting to warm up to him. After all, he was going to be in our lives forever because of our new baby.

We smiled and talked about the future. There was so much hope. Rashad was planning to get his GED. I was on my way to college. We had a baby on the way. Everybody was getting along. Life was perfect. Yet, I still couldn't ignore the strange feeling that settled deep inside of me like a dull ache.

When I ate, Nadia was always more active than usual, but this was the second time today that I didn't feel a kick or elbow press against my protruding belly. Although worried, I tried to stay calm and focused on more positive things like seeing our beautiful baby for the first time, if induced early.

While awaiting the good news, the doctor finally knocked on the door and entered.

Right on schedule, I thought.

My hands were achy, and those faithful grasshoppers leaped in my belly— an overpowering reminder of love growing inside of me. Massaging my hands together to calm my nerves, I lie back on the table, and lifted my shirt to hear my daughter's heartbeat. This was my favorite part of having a prenatal check-up— hearing my unborn child's heartbeat.

This is it. We'll finally get to see her, I thought. *She'll be in our arms soon.*

We couldn't wait to meet Nadia.

The doctor squeezed a glob of blue jelly into his gloved hand, rubbed it on my stomach, and pressed the heart monitor against my skin, rotating it in a circular motion. However, as we waited a couple of minutes for the sound of a pulsating heartbeat, an overwhelming silence filled the room.

"Something's wrong with the monitor," explained the doctor tapping it in his hand. "Let me try a different one."

I tried my best not to worry as the nurse brought in a second monitor.

Silence. No heartbeat.

May Showers

When it rains, it pours.

We did everything right. I had a full, healthy nine months of pregnancy. We made plans. We had three baby showers. We were ready, but not for what had happened.

A thousand invisible eyes were staring me right in the face. The clinical grey hospital room was sterile and lifeless. I could feel something different even before they told me what I prayed wouldn't be true. For nine months, I carried Nadia. Now, she was gone.

"I'm so sorry for your loss," said the doctor.

I didn't want anyone to feel sorry for me. I wanted to hear her heartbeat on that monitor and watch it flutter like a little butterfly again. I wanted to feel the little hiccups on the lower left side of my abdomen as I pressed down lightly on the area and smiled. But most of all, I wanted my daughter back.

Why me, Lord? I asked, silently. I needed answers.

Momma wrapped her arms around me. A strange and strangled sound escaped from my lungs. Rashad sat in a chair, holding his head in his hands as tears fell into his lap.

"She was too good for this world," explained Momma explained in a soothing tone while rubbing my hair and holding back her own tears. "She wasn't meant to be on this earth. Her heart is beating in heaven."

Momma's words of comfort sat with us but had not made it into our hearts yet.

How could this happen? Why did this happen? This can't be real. This isn't real. This isn't real.

Innumerable tears poured out of me like a thunderstorm. Our daughter was inside of me— she lived there, and she died there.

Darkness draped over my shoulders like a cloak. This pain was brand new and fresh. It would take many years to recover and heal.

Before the Storm

"You can go home and wait for your water to naturally break," explained the doctor. "Or, we can induce you for an early labor and delivery."

What? I thought. I couldn't believe that going home was an option. It just didn't make sense. *Why would I go home?*

Momma spoke for me, "No, we want her to have the baby tonight since the baby is no longer with us anymore."

I found a bit of strength to back up Momma. "I'm staying right here and having my baby," I told the doctor. I wasn't going anywhere until Nadia was delivered.

While we waited for the nurse to give me the epidural to start labor, Momma called all the family to the hospital for support. Within the hour, both of our families were notified and by our side. Even my biological father Thomas and older brother Marquis were on their way from Detroit and Kansas City.

Family members took turns coming into the room to offer their condolences while Rashad stood at my bedside, holding my hand. No matter the encouragement that visitors offered, this was a pain that no one could sooth.

We silently searched each other's faces for answers. No words could express the amount of devastation and turmoil that we felt.

This can't be real. This can't be happening. Am I dreaming? It felt like a dream, but we were awake. This nightmare was real. *Why did this happen? How did this happen? Why us?*

All we could do was search for understanding in each other's arms.

Family War

As family from all sides filled the hospital room, Momma prayed and offered comforting words to help make sense of this unexpected loss.

"God does everything for a reason. Some things happen that are out of our control, but God knows what's best and he does all things well," said Momma. "We're going to move forward."

Many family members added in an "Amen," "Yes," and "Jesus," throughout the speech but all I could feel was an overwhelming numbness.

As I lie in the hospital bed, I couldn't move. I was frozen. All I could do was stare back at Ms. Katina whose cold eyes sat above the bed rail, at the foot of my bed. Her glare cut me open even before the doctor could. She had a look that I would never forget— dark and scornful. Her eyes were piercing. A silent war was brewing between the families that only God would have the ability to resolve.

"I'm thirsty," I said in a low tone. The nurses instructed me not to drink anything before the epidural, but that had been hours ago.

"You can drink some water," said Ms. Katina.

"Can't nobody pregnant drink water before they have the baby," said Momma. "They usually give the mother ice chips. I'll go check though. Maybe they'll give her a popsicle."

"She can't eat no popsicle," replied Ms. Katina. I done had all these babies. I know that baby can drink water."

"I ain't never heard of that," Momma didn't agree. She felt like she knew what was best for me and believed that Ms. Katina had no say in telling her how to raise her daughter, especially since she had allowed me to go over to her house when I wasn't even allowed to be there.

"*My* daughter can't drink no water before she has the baby," Momma continued, "But I'll go find out."

I could tell my Momma and Rashad's Momma were getting on each other's nerves. It was no secret that they didn't really like each other. They were just putting up with each other for the sake of me, Rashad, and the baby. However, drama was the last thing we needed to focus on at a time like this.

I looked at Rashad who was standing next to me. I hoped he would say something to diffuse the situation, but he just shook his head from side-to-side and looked down.

To help keep the peace, Momma continued to offer comforting words to help calm everybody's nerves. She spoke aloud to everyone in the room.

"We're going to be behind Jenesis and Rashad during this time," said Momma.

However, as Momma spoke, Ms. Katina shared something with her sisters loud enough for everyone to hear.

"I can't stand that Bitch," said Ms. Katina.

Momma caught wind of what she said, held her composure, and without batting an eye, finished her speech, "And in conclusion, I don't even like you either."

Both mothers stared each other down, until Momma walked out of the room to pull the nurse aside to speak with her about the ice chips and to alert her of what was going on.

"I feel like some stuff is about to go down and I want everyone out of the room," said Momma. "My daughter is going through a lot right now and we can't have this. That woman just called me out of my name."

The nurse agreed to bring security into the room, but he didn't come fast enough.

When Momma returned to the room with the ice chips, she addressed Ms. Katina

"Did you call me a Bitch?"

"Yeah, I called you a Bitch," said Ms. Katina.

Momma replied back, "Who you callin' a bitch? A bitch is a person you can't control. We can talk about it outside this room."

Monique stepped in to defend her mother. "You're not gonna talk to my Momma like that!"

The room was getting heated and so was everyone in there.

"When Rashad was in your house, he should've killed you," said Ms. Katina.

One word led to another, and before we knew it, both sides of the family were ready to scrap. It was about to be a showdown in the hospital room. Everybody was ready to fight. The whole thing was a big mess.

Thankfully, security arrived, and all visitors were cleared out of the room except Momma, Grandma, and Rashad. However, Rashad was upset and in defense mode.

"Why you talk about my Momma like that, Ms. Karen?" asked Rashad.

Rashad loved his Momma unconditionally. She could do no wrong in his eyes. However, she was plain wrong for calling *my* Momma out of her name. I couldn't believe he was taking his Momma's side when she started the whole thing. I loved Rashad, but I hated what was going. He should have helped to diffuse the situation, but he didn't.

"You know what," said Momma addressing Rashad. "I'm sorry for disrespecting your Momma. And I'm sorry your Momma disrespected my daughter. This is a time when the family needs to be close not farther from each other."

She was right. After all that had happened, we needed to pull ourselves together. The day was already long and painful. It was a hard day for both families.

Labor and Delivery

May 19th. 1:05am. I was in labor for nine hours. Those hours felt like years. My stomach sunk deeper into itself. I felt hollow. But now, it was time to deliver Nadia.

"Would you like to have a mirror at the foot of the bed?" asked the doctor who motioned to a tall, standing mirror in the corner of the room.

"Yes," I quickly responded. "I want to see her. I want to see everything."

As painful as it was to have witnessed the birth of my daughter, any memory of her was paramount to my healing. Our time together was precious, delicate, but limited.

***

"1, 2, 3, push..." instructed the doctor.

Holding my breath, the contractions were coming more frequently. My muscles tightened as I strained and pushed as hard as I could through the pressure. I was determined to see my daughter's face.

"She's crowning," said the doctor.

That was all the encouragement I needed. I didn't need instructions or a countdown. I closed my eyes, squeezed my muscles, pushed harder, and looked into the mirror. I saw a head full of black curly hair.

"You're doing good," said the nurse. "1, 2, 3, push."

I squeezed and pressed down as hard as I could one final time. When I raised my eyes to the mirror, I saw my daughter's limp and lifeless body, in fetal position, exit my womb.

Her face was purple from the umbilical cord that was wrapped around her neck twice. I gasped, at the sight, wondering if that was the reason for her passing. All kinds of thoughts flooded my mind. I would later find out that although the umbilical cord was wrapped around her neck, that wasn't the cause of my daughter's death.

"The baby is out," said the doctor, unwrapping the umbilical cord from around her neck. "Good job."

The doctor carefully moved Nadia from my bedside to the preparation table for the nurse to wash her. Lying there, I admired my daughter's beauty.

"She is perfect," I said.

Unlike normal labor and delivery stories, the comforting relief of hearing the cries of a baby just born to ease all worry of a new parent was absent. There was only silence. Nadia had arrived into this world as what the doctor's named stillborn. But she had always been my angel then, and even before the transition. Nothing would ever change that.

Through Nana's Eyes

I'll never forget it. We packed the hospital bag in preparation for the baby to come home. We had everything in there— lotion, baby powder, diapers, and her first outfit.

After my daughter gave birth to Nadia, I cut the umbilical cord. Rashad asked me to. When my daughter needed him the most, he wasn't there. The whole time my daughter was giving birth, he stood in the corner of the room and faced the wall. So, I had the honor of cutting my first granddaughter's umbilical cord.

Once Nadia arrived, the nurses washed her up and afterwards, asked me, "Do you want to clean her up?"

"Yeah," I said. I looked over at the red bag that we packed with all the pregnant stuff that we were so excited about the day before. Everything happened so fast.

While standing with the nurses, I looked at Nadia from under the bright hospital light and helped the nurses.

"What does she look like?" asked Jenesis. She lifted up from the bed to get a better view.

"Jenesis, she is so beautiful."

I examined my grandchild from head to toe. I noticed a little blister on her leg and near her foot. "Where is that from?" I asked the nurse.

"It's from her being in the uterus," she said. "Her body was absorbing the water."

I looked at her little big toe— a family signature. I couldn't help but smile. I looked at her nails. She was so cute. I cleaned her and put baby powder on her.

"Can I put lotion on her?" I asked the nurse.

"Yeah, you can put lotion on her," the nurse replied.

With tears in my eyes, I dressed her in her Winnie the Pooh sleeper and combed her beautiful hair. See, in our family, the women have silky, black hair, and so did Nadia. I wrapped her up in a tiny blanket and brought her over to my daughter.

As I placed Nadia in her arms, my daughter looked at her baby and said, "You are so beautiful and so perfect. I will never let you go."

Tears poured down her cheeks as she looked at me and spoke.

"She is so beautiful, Momma. I did all the right stuff. I ate turkey sandwiches, drank smoothies…"

"There was nothing wrong that you done, Jenesis," I said.

My daughter had lost a child, and for the first time in my daughter's life, I couldn't make it right. There was nothing I could do. I felt worthless and powerless. I wished I could change what had happened, but all I could do was watch and pray.

Through Rashad's Eyes

I was at my lowest that I had ever been. I felt so weak. I thought I had it all together, but when we lost Nadia, my whole world crumbled. She was my everything.

The only thing that I had left to hold onto was Jenesis. I just couldn't lose her. She was the only person who believed in me.

Although, I had my family, I needed more. I needed Jenesis. She was the only person I could open up to. She knew the struggles that I was going through. She understood me in a way that no one else did. When I didn't know who to turn to, Jenesis was always there. But I knew things would soon change. She was on her way to college. I was still in the streets. It was just a matter of time before she would leave me. The thought was unbearable.

I didn't have faith at the time. I didn't know how to pray. So, I did what any lost person would— I blamed God for what he had done. This was His fault. And I blamed myself.

How could this happen? Why would this happen? I thought. I felt even more like a failure. Flashbacks of my daughter's lifeless body exiting the womb haunted me. In the hospital room, I couldn't even stand there and cut my daughter's umbilical cord. Instead, I turned my head and let Ms. Karen do it.

My heart just couldn't take it. It felt like a butcher knife was digging into it every time I thought of my daughter. I wanted to die. For the first time in my life, I really felt like life was not worth living. I had struggled with depression and suicidal thoughts in the past, but this was the worst I had ever experienced. I had lost Nadia. Now, I was losing myself.

that day

the murmur of
"my daughter is not gone."
seeps from my lips
my womb is sinking.

Asphyxiate. Bottomless.
And Raw.
Excretion of soul
scream.
shudder.
scream.
quiet.

Motions are paused
slowly understood
interlock of memory palms
a lukewarm prayer.

"What God?"

demons flew from his nose
onto my lap
each one, dancing with bells. Ruby

and tender to
heart dissipation.
Black oil,
streaking
melon ripe cheeks.

They know.

The knees collapse
The neck extends with lines
The fingers have stiffened
The torso has curved
The body jerks blindly
The tongue is bleeding
The open mouth is dark
The voice is voiceless.

the child has died
as i
caress the uterus.
it
shifted
and
fell
before
i
could
catch

it

"Momma loves her baby girl." I told her.
"Don't leave me…"
She remained still.
I held
that child
alone

Mode

the room grew cold
as her skin
the room darkened
as her skin
crease of my forehead thickened

cracking oil inside my face

Fingers are webbed together
I grip her firmly and close.
Breasts full with birth milk roped
I brush my warm cheek against my daughter's

"Why not me Lord?"

hoping for an answer.
Breath

Breathing
I am alive.
And
I
Remember.

A Reason in Every Season

The hospital room was quiet. It was just me, the baby, Rashad, and Momma in there. Silence and hospital monitors were the only noise in the room. I held my daughter in my arms and close to my heart. The sweet scent of fresh, ripe strawberries was perfume on her skin. That was her natural scent from all the fruit I ate throughout the pregnancy.

Why did this happen? Did I do something wrong? Could this have been prevented?

We wanted answers. So, when I requested an autopsy, that's what we expected. But when the autopsy report arrived, there were none. Nadia was a completely healthy, full-term baby. Nothing was wrong. The umbilical cord was not the cause of death. It just didn't make sense. I read, re-read, tried to decode and decipher the medical jargon, and skimmed the report up and down several times for answers but there were none.

The doctor stood by the hospital bed and offered the best explanation that he possibly could.

"This is a beautiful child," he said. "This is due to natural causes. Some things are unexplainable. Some things don't have a reason. But she's perfect."

As the doctor walked out of the room, Momma wrapped her love and wisdom wrapped around me.

"She's perfectly at peace," said Momma. "She's not with us anymore. Something that never hurt nobody. Something that never bothered nobody just didn't make it. But I believe that God does *everything* for a reason. We can't question God. It's just all in his will."

I cried in Momma's arms.

"Nadia is with us in a different way," she said. "In spirit."

Visitation

God never left my side. And my family— the people in my life who were there for me— gave their time, energy, comforting words, cards, balloons, flowers, and sympathy. However, when my eleven-year-old brother Christopher walked into the hospital room, I wasn't prepared for his reaction. He didn't understand. He walked up to the bed as I held Nadia in my arms.

"What happened?" asked Christopher with a sad and confused look on his face. "What happened to the baby?"

No one had told him yet. How could we? I didn't know what to say or even how to say it. I knew how much he loved his niece. I couldn't find the words to explain to him what happened. Thankfully, our mother stepped in and spoke for me.

"She didn't make it," said Momma with tears in her eyes.

"Why?" he cried. "I bought her that outfit." His tears fell heavy onto his jacket.

We held each other in that small hospital room. Me, Momma, Christopher, an angel, and God.

The Damage was Done

That morning, I moved to the maternity ward with Nadia in my arms. As I held her for the last final moments, Momma briefly stepped out of the room leaving me and my baby alone to bond. That's when my words came for the first time.

"God, take me and bring my daughter back," I said aloud. I looked around the dimly lit room, I noticed cards, a vase with pink roses, balloons, the "It's a girl" sign, and I cried.

I did everything right during my pregnancy. Why did God choose me to go through this? My thoughts floated around us making the room darker. Yet, there remained a glimmer of light.

While Momma was outside of the room, she walked down the hallway and there stood the nurse from the doctor's office who refused to do the ultrasound because we had misplaced the pink and blue belts. Momma approached the nurse in the hallway with a straight face. The nurse recognized her.

"Oh, I remember you," the nurse said emotionless. "How's your daughter doing?"

Momma's eyes were ice cold as she stared at her, but her voice was warm.

"She's fine," replied Momma. "She had the baby."

Silence filled the space between them. Momma continued, "You want to go see her?"

"Yeah," replied the nurse.

"Come down here," Momma said, guiding her down the hallway to the room.

"I can't wait to see her," said the nurse.

"She'll be glad to see *you*," replied Momma.

When the nurse walked into the room, she was stunned.

"What happened?" she asked.

"The baby is stillborn," said Momma, calculatedly. She looked from the nurse to me and Nadia. "She didn't make it. My daughter's really hurt. It's going to be a while before she recovers from this."

The nurse looked at me, holding Nadia in my arms without saying a word.

But Momma had something else to say.

"You know what?" asked Momma, turning to the nurse. "Maybe, if you were a little nicer that day and would have given her those belts for the ultrasound, maybe we could have caught this in time. So, maybe this is your fault." She continued, "So, how do you think my daughter feels right now?"

The nurse's eyes grew the size of two golf balls as she put her hands against her distraught face, cried, and ran out of the room into the hallway, knocking stuff over. But the damage had already been done. The pain had been caused. And a life had been taken.

The room sat quiet. It would take many years for the raw wound to be sealed and healed. It was the worst day we had ever experienced.

Letting Go

Nadia was a beautiful baby. The hospital gave me a gift with items that belonged to her—a turquoise keepsake box that was tied with a white ribbon. This memory box held a lock of Nadia's hair, her footprints, an unofficial birth certificate, and photos of her in the dress that she was supposed to arrive home in.

The first couple of days, Nadia arrived in a plexiglass bassinet carrier designed for newborns. On the third and fourth days, the Chaplain carried her into the room in a bassinet-sized metal carrier. As Nadia was placed in my arms, I noticed that her skin was colder than normal.

"We need to warm her," I said. My first reaction was of a nurturing mother. We turned the heat up in the room. However, as I held and kissed Nadia, drops of blood escaped her nose. She had been gone and in my arms for four days.

"It's time to let go, baby," explained Momma. "Dig deep inside of yourself and find the same love that you carried Nadia with and use that for your strength."

Losing Poetry

No words could express the amount of pain that I felt. I was floating in the deep-sea of my tears. Every time I came up for air, a massive wave hit me. I didn't know how I was going to survive. I was sinking.

People tried to make it better. Words. Cards. Flowers. Hugs. This was a pain that I never imagined feeling. It was a new and fresh wound. But it was time to make the funeral arrangements, and I had to think about that now. I was drowning in my thoughts until I heard Momma speak.

"Baby, you can write a poem to read at the funeral," explained Momma. She had never seen her daughter in such a depressed and fragile state of mind and condition.

What would I say? What could I write about that would make this all better? I wondered.

Although I couldn't find the words to express all that I felt, I found the strength to write a poem for my daughter. So many words came to me all at once. I didn't know where to start. Overwhelmed, I put the pencil down, closed my eyes, and cried.

Heavy teardrops fell and soaked the paper. It was my first time writing since before finding out that I was pregnant. Nadia was my poetry. But now, I had to write a poem for my daughter's funeral. Wiping my tears and picking up the pencil, it was the first time that I had ever lost poetry.

Untitled

I made sure I held you to the very end
God knows my heart
left when you did
but I held on
to the very
end
and
I'll never
let go.

Forgotten Toys

While in the hospital, we prepared for the next steps for my granddaughter's homegoing ceremony. As we made plans, I went to various second-hand stores in search of a bassinet-styled basket.

"Let me show you what we have in the back," said the saleswoman who guided Momma through the store.

Toys were everywhere and piled on the floor in the corner. These were toys that children had played with, gave away, and forgotten about. Somebody's kids had played with and loved on those toys. But now they were there for another child to own. My grandbaby will never have the opportunity to play with any of these toys— whether new or old, I thought.

As I looked at the toys, I started to cry. I couldn't even give those toys to my grandchild. My heart was bleeding.

Walking further through the store, more toys were scattered from one end of the store to the other. There were so many. But as I looked further back in the room, there it was— a basket-woven bassinet. It was perfect for Nadia's homegoing ceremony and visitation service.

The Homegoing of Nadia Michelle Robinson
HOPE WITH GOD

Hope is so strong
In me as the light,
In turn became the life in me,
Allowing me to become a nurturer,
Developer, friend- but most of all mother.

With every thought, feeling, emotion
Passed, she knew me deeply
As one never has.

So strong is hope
Her pulsing heart pumped
Vibrating to every stride I made
To accomplish my life for her own.

Her soul was the finest entity of existence

Strong is my Hope,
My little, sweet love,
The baby that we created
My heart, that now lives above

The Funeral

Scene I.
Parched lilies groped
nape of neck,
peeling away, layered trembles-
the leaves
tremble and quake,
softening the verbs
of loved ones-
the soul begins to play
and so does my child,
cornering the array.
I glimpse,
her physic
positioned.
Her complexion,
now bronze,
sweetness
overshadowed by rank
powder, not created for new light,
but sharp pains
plummet portraits,
still life.
Sounds, allay as
sight is sustained.
Amble narrowly toward core,
the soul wilts.

they are humming behind ramparts
they are humming behind coated paint.
Behind the odor
I hear
Smiling faces
the absurdity.

they pause, but shortly begin twice.
(sighing)

Knocking down the boarded floor,
And, so does the soul.
Spreading doves
on wilting lilies
and, it is then,
He enters.

Scene II.
Holding his face in place
"Ooooooh-
da bay-bee."

His voice on piano keys and years
worn clothes
dismantled hair uncombed
He moans.
And he's doing all of this
by my baby

by
my
little
sweet
baby.

"Excuse me, sir. This is a private awake."
From my mother's lips.

*"I jus' wanna see da bay-bee.
She so bu-tiful."*

Walking toward he
who seems
to know my child.
Love,
holds my hand.

I glance. At the man
I glance. At his vertical stance

moving slowly toward the horizontal basket
I watch the peaceful child
Lifting from the flowered basket
bright almond-eyed pitted
she too can speak with a face of five years age

"Look, mommy. We bof' dress togeder- in pink."

Joyful in my spirit. I say,
"I know little sugar.
You'll always be my little sweet thang."

She smiles a smile of life
but she is not.

alive.

no longer, is she

alive.

And I hold tightly to love's hand.
Recalling, the old man

Scene III
who gravely approaches,
looking below at the child.
Whose body is closed.
When his soul begins to play.

Humming inside the walls
of parched lilies
that grope nape of neck bend.
My bones tremble.
His soul wilts.

But the lilies still accrue.
Pink and white flower petals
lilac doves
singing.
The old man's hands
His fingers crooked and black.
He cries,

"But Why me, Lord?
I am afraid."

Humming.
Please
strengthen the
pain.
And, for once,
the old man proclaims,

"Child, Oh, my child.
She will return,
refocus your plan,
and she will return.
For you."

Cradling the child,
The old man walks,
carrying the child
towards the wall.

It is where the humming began.

She never lets go. Clutching to his cloak,
baby eyes watch me from his frail-hungry
shoulders
two pair of massive wings engulf the funeral

my child is alive,

my child is alive,

Again.

High School Graduation

On May 25, I didn't think I had the strength to walk across the graduation stage wearing a white cap and gown to receive my high school diploma, but I did.

I wore all white— a satin and lace spaghetti-strap blouse, wide-legged pinstripe capris, and black and white pinstripe heels. My step-sister and biological father took me shopping for this special occasion. It had been an unexpected long week and they wanted to cheer me up before the big ceremony.

While I managed to smile a few times, my thoughts went right back to Nadia. When I felt a ting of happiness, I felt guilty. I was still mourning.

Momma parked in front of the building where the graduation ceremony was being held with the car flashers on. Staring out the window, I could see my classmates— the other graduates who were getting dropped off to line-up by their last names for the processional like me. However, as the time grew closer for the ceremony to begin, I felt nauseous.

Even though I had worked so hard from Kindergarten to 12th grade to finally graduate, the ceremony was the last thing on my mind. My daughter was gone and there was no way that I could bring her back.

"I don't want to go in there," I told Momma. Tears sat heavy in my eyes. "I don't want anyone feeling sorry for me. I don't want anyone to say anything about the baby. I don't want to talk about it." Tears streamed down my cheeks.

"You can do this," said Momma. "You've worked so hard and you've come this far. You are strong. Do this for Nadia."

I bowed my head as tears fell into my lap, leaving wet, translucent puddles on my graduation gown.

"Reach inside yourself and pull out that same love that you have for your baby and use it for yourself right now," said Momma. "Put one foot in front of the other and don't look back."

The bright sun spilled into the windows of the car as Momma's soothing voice filled the space. Momma's words were strong and powerful.

She continued, "You're gonna start feeling the sun on your face and being happy again. You're not going to forget about her but you're going to learn to live with the pain. The pain don't go away you just learn to live with it.

What don't kill you will only make you stronger."

Nodding to Momma, I wiped my tears, and found the strength to step out of the car.

Standing in front of the building, I straightened and smoothed out my graduation gown until a quick gust of wind blew my white cap to the sidewalk. Hurriedly, I tried to grab it before it got dirty, but another graduate picked it up and handed it to me.

As I received the cap from her and said thank you, her eyes told me that she was sorry for my loss. Those words that everyone says because they don't know what else to say, or when there is nothing else to say.

After entering the building, every time I glanced at somebody, I was met with the same look— they felt sorry for me. I didn't want anyone feeling sorry for me. I wanted everything to be normal again.

Some of my friends greeted me with hugs. People who performed with me in marching band. People who read urban love stories with me. People who sat with me in the school cafeteria. People who had class with me. People who I cared about and loved. I didn't know what to say. No words could express the insurmountable agony that I felt. But they already knew. It had been a week since our senior trip, and I was pregnant last time they saw me. They were sad for my loss. I felt ashamed, embarrassed, and humiliated.

Although my daughter's death was out of my control, I had lost her. I didn't know how they found out or even how much they knew about but none of that mattered. All I knew was everything hurt, and no one knew the rawness of it.

Why did this happen? I wondered. *I'm supposed to be happy on this day.*

All that I had felt and seen over the past few days was etched on my memory, hovering over me like a spirit. Half of me was present for my graduation but the other half was missing. I had lost the only thing that mattered most to me. And I didn't have anything to show for it.

I was silently breaking in the graduation stands but thankful to be sitting next to my best friend, Stephanie. She had visited me a few times in the hospital and even got a chance to see Nadia in my arms. That kind of friendship is precious and priceless.

While waiting for our names to be called, I reached into the pocket of my graduation robe for my favorite picture of Nadia.

As tears hit the photo, Stephanie held and squeezed my hand.

"When they call my name, I'm going to walk across the stage and hold up this picture," I whispered to Stephanie. "I want everyone to see my baby."

When the Assistant Principal announced my name, it felt surreal. Walking across the stage, I held my daughter's picture in the air as my family cheered. All I could see past my tears was Momma smiling and waving Nadia's pink teddy bear in the air. And that's just what I needed— hope.

**

After the ceremony, my family greeted me among a crowd of other graduates and their families.

"I am so proud of you!" said Momma. "You did it!"

The warm and loving arms of my family surrounded me. They knew what I was going through. However, as I celebrated with my family, I couldn't help but notice Rashad who stood off to the side of the crowd with his hands in his jean's pockets, deep in his thoughts.

I was able to catch his eyes and smile, only to be met with a half-smile that made his eyes darker. Trying to stay positive, I walked with my family to the front entrance where Cousin Robert pulled up unexpectedly on his brand-new cobalt blue motorcycle.

"Get on, Apple Head," he said smiling and handing me a helmet. "I'm taking you for a ride!"

Putting on my helmet, I hopped on the back of Cousin Robert's motorcycle, holding tightly to his waist.

"Hold on!" he said, before speeding off down the street as everyone waved goodbye.

Resting against his jacket, the cool breeze blew tears across my face and the wind wisped long, straight hair strands all around me. Looking out into the unknown distance, I knew the road that lie ahead of me was going to be long and hard. I didn't know how I was going to get there or where I would end up. Uncertainty and doubt settled in until Momma's wise words from past talks echoed in my mind, "Life is a choice. You can make it good, or you can make it bad. It's all up to you."

Although the road that lie ahead was unclear, there was one thing that I knew for sure, and that was, no matter my decision: I was determined to survive despite my obstacles.

"God has a purpose and a plan for your life," said many wise people.

Words of encouragement helped clear the fog. However, I didn't know exactly what God had planned for me and that was what scared me the most.

Scholarship

in hand
stride toward the stairwell
everybody clapping

Bourgeoisie.

Impoverished.

Comfortable.

Invisible.

And the motion is slow whispers and a sudden
pause accepted.
in pulse
solitary light. The dress is elegant
delicate symbol fabric, but
not that long until
lips grew tight and the
eyes had questions.

"How could you let this happen?"

drop on the bed edge

that night,

before
my tongue on edge and couldn't utter
one single

"Sorry, Momma."

already been too late.
three brushes with the_____
for a couple years.
just too damn late-
by the sink.

Positive

stripe oriental pink that evening
for the celebration,
but just couldn't break the given.
eyes that had given words
couldn't answer at all.

Can't even speak to my Momma, so why you
trippin?

i shake it off.

I got the damn award didn't I?

but that

don't make me
no nevuh mind.

*"She got HIS baby in her-
now, ain't that somethin positive."*

and I am neglected
because
i chose to love so young
i chose to make love so young

Am I so wrong?

no.
at least, not yet.

i just found out how to change the epitome of
negativity.
I am certain there is an answer for all of this-
some kind of explanation because
i still
got this scholarship in my hand.
and,
i still
got this child's fingers in my ribs.
now
who gonna answer me when i finally…

"He will." pointed
to the absent father who
reads behind one yellow shade
with one mattress in
six digits.

but he can't.
he lives inside
my child's cell
and mine. i breathe life into both cords.
and. and.
i am wearing pink this evening.
broke away from the finger-hand and ran.
Could not stop my stride toward the stairway.
everything is just so damn bright
and inside my pupils
and inside my head
and behind my child.

JUST
STOP

i want to just stop the whispers and, yes,
a baby is out in the audience dark,
can't see the face but the whimper is there,
you know,
the baby-cries that
have not made it yet,

and the mother,
she has not received her apology yet.

i tried Momma. i tried to explain,
see me Momma, for the very first time
as you have seen me for the very first time.
but listen,
this child won't see these eyes,
and this child
that
is
inside, is clutching me,
wanting me to hold so tightly
but my fingers have been bloody once before,

see this time,
but i can't take no more.
and, i can't take no more awards.

so
i've made the decision since they knew all
along,
nevuh been so positive in all my life.
lost the hand the scholarship held
when the grip broke
and the neck fell back
and my neck fell back

and nothing.
nothing. was left
though
one cord was broken,
with the other one

intact.

Keep Hope

They told me to Keep Hope,
so I laid my body down without sound for him.
Even though my past haunted me
walking me stiffly to unknown closets-
unknown hurt. Pain flowing as yesterday's tears
and tomorrows, but to Keep Hope
I laid my body down.

"Keep Hope," he told me.
Dream upon the sky far from the nightmares,
now, open your eyes.
Remember, they persecuted me
they will also persecute you.
They degraded me, so to Keep Hope,
I made one step further with Hope.

As I keep Hope,
energy drained from my body.
I could no longer, imagine suffering,
It imagined me.
With every breath mirrored to me,
I pushed and I watched
I pushed and I watched
"1, 2, 3 and push." I pushed and I watched,
and I saw Hope, but Hope didn't see me
to tell me- Keep

Part SIX

Break the Cycle

Moving Out

In a span of three months, when I was eighteen years old, I had lost Nadia, moved out of Momma's house, rented an apartment, and went off to college. Everything happened so fast.

My first apartment was a gothic, grey stone building. Every type of person lived in this complex— school drop-outs, college students, single mothers, married couples, prostitutes, and drug dealers.

I grew up hearing how hard it was to be an adult.

"Enjoy your childhood while you can," I'd often hear people say.

And they weren't playing about that either. When I moved out of Momma's house, I learned the true meaning of being grown. It was definitely more than turning eighteen and leaving your Momma's house. Being a grown up meant that I had bills to pay and responsibilities to handle on my own. However, I still enjoyed all the perks of having my own place.

I decorated my apartment like an art gallery with colorful pictures and minimal furniture to compliment the glass French doors and mahogany wood floors that were polished so well that you could see your reflection. I needed a living space that would help inspire my writing and creative expression again, especially since me and Rashad's relationship was taking an abrupt turn for the worst. He seemed different, but I just couldn't put my finger on it.

Red Flags

The fire between Rashad and I burned strong and long, but I had yet to feel its flames. I hadn't seen how large it could grow. Just with one spark, the fire became massive and overpowering. It burned down everything leaving damage, rubbish, and ash behind. I couldn't let it consume me. I had to extinguish it. It was a matter of life or death. We were wrapped up in each other, but he just wouldn't let me go.

***

During my first semester of college Rashad's insecurities fueled the anger that lie dormant inside of him. I looked forward to my new status as a college student and everything that came with it. However, as I shared my innermost dreams and goals with Rashad, a dark and vacant expression spread across his face as he seemed to imagine all the things that could go wrong with us.

"You're in college," explained Rashad. "You're gonna find somebody else."

"Baby, I will never do that," I explained. "What are you talking about? Where's this coming from?"

Ignoring my question, he assumed the worst.

"You're not gonna stay with me," he insisted. "Look at me, Jenesis! I'm nothing. You're gonna leave me. I know you will."

"That won't happen," I promised. "I won't leave you."

This vow seemed to ease Rashad's mind, as his tone softened and became less aggressive, changing his demeanor.

"I love you so much," he said, staring into my eyes, grabbing my hands, and pulling me close to his body. "Don't ever leave me. I need you and can't lose you."

A warm sensation traveled through me.

"I love you with all my heart and I promise, I'm not going anywhere," I whispered.

No one ever said, "I love you," like Rashad.

He really means it, I thought. *I need him, too.*

An Emotional Rollercoaster

Insecurity, low self-esteem, anti-social, controlling, aggressive, uncontrollable anger, and depression— these features of Rashad's character were red flags and warning signs of an unhealthy relationship that I ignored.

"If you look at another man, that's cheating," said Rashad.

I didn't know much about relationships at the time so when he told me that, I believed him. I would later realize that it was really just a way for him to control me. Moreover, while there was no justification for Rashad to question my affection, cheating accusations happened frequently. As a result, I quickly learned to avoid all eye contact with men and looked down at the ground even though I wasn't a cheater.

When we were finally alone, I asked, "Why do you always accuse me of things that I don't do?"

"You're the kind of girl who every boy wants," said Rashad. I'm not attractive. I'm a dropout. I don't have nothin'. You can have anybody. Why do you want me?"

"Because I love you," I told him genuinely.

But Rashad didn't hear me. All he could hear were his own negative thoughts.

A shadow of the world

Sitting there
hair covering my face
the evening sun
shadowing through strands of
hair.

My face.
swollen
pain.

lifting my weight
to the squeeky concrete floor
I make it to the
big dusty mirror.
I watch
I cry with pain of
unwanted secrets.
will these secrets come out?
will this story ever end?
Why me?
Why me?
why me?

An Unhealthy Relationship

My heart was leading me to places that I never thought I would find myself in. I was utterly lost. Even my own reflection was unrecognizable.

Everyone including Momma gave me advice about leaving Rashad, but I didn't listen.

"He ain't no good," said Momma. "You can do better, and I want better for you. I just don't understand why you're with him."

I heard Momma's voice, but I wasn't listening. My mind was somewhere far away. I didn't think Momma understood what I was going through. But little did I know, her age brought maturity and wisdom through experience that people my age just didn't possess. I should have listened to Momma when she was telling me things. I was just too stubborn to do so.

"This ain't my first rodeo," explained Momma. "I've been around the block a few times and a zebra can't change its stripes, baby."

No matter how much Momma or anybody else tried to talk some sense into me, I thought I was in love. I guess love can sometimes be blind if you choose to keep your eyes closed.

Love is Blind

Advice came from all directions— some I listened to, some I didn't. Regardless, my patience was dwindling. Constantly reaffirming my affection for Rashad was exhausting. I was getting tired of all the false accusations from his insecurities.

"You don't love me," he said. "You're gonna find somebody else and leave me."

"I'll never do that," I insisted. "Why do you keep saying this. I'm in love with you."

Rashad never listened. He was becoming more negative by the day. I tried my best to console him, but it always backfired.

"Stop saying that!" he responded. "You don't love me, and I don't believe you."

It was a never-ending cycle of violence. Furthermore, as I attempted to calm and affirm my love for him, Rashad's eyes shifted wildly, as anger covered his face.

"I hate myself. I hate being me. I just wanna die," explained Rashad. "I'm gonna kill myself!"

I felt hopeless and trapped in a cycle of self-loathing. As much as I wanted our relationship to work, the constant talk about suicide was a reminder that Rashad couldn't possibly be in love with me.

Momma's words from past talks echoed in my mind at times like this.

"If someone doesn't love and care about themselves and life, how can you expect them to love and care about yours?"

Rashad knew how to make me forget Momma's wisdom when he did exactly what he always did— apologized.

"I'm sorry baby," he said. "I didn't mean it. Please forgive me. I love you. I don't wanna lose you."

These were the apologies that he offered after a fight. I forgave him like always. I thought that his jealous and overprotective ways were a sign of love, but they were really a sign of manipulation. We would break up, then get back together again. I was a passenger on Rashad's emotional rollercoaster.

After fights, I searched his eyes for any sign of love and remorse for his actions, but all I could see was pain, depression, anger, and confusion. They say the eyes are the windows to the soul, but I was in denial.

"He's gonna change," I said, trying to convince the people around me to support the relationship. "He's different now. Everything is okay— I'm okay."

These were all falsities that I told family and friends as I used every excuse in the book to protect his flawed character. However, the reality was, we just couldn't love each other the right way, and as this realization became clearer, it wasn't long before I finally took off the mask and told the truth.

Stephanie

My best friend could see past the mask and excuses that I used to hide the abuse. She was the only person who I could really talk to about my problems. She had my back and I had hers. So, one day, over the phone, I finally told Stephanie everything.

"You need to make up in your mind that you're going to leave him for good," she said.

At first, I was having conflicting thoughts about breaking up with Rashad, but now my mind was made up. This time, I was serious and really wanted to walk away, but I knew how much of a temper he had, and I was afraid of how Rashad would react. I had seen him violent and was not sure how far it could go. I didn't plan on sticking around to find out.

"I can't do this anymore," I told her.

"You need to leave him then," said Stephanie.

But some things are easier said than done. I had been in a relationship with Rashad for five years, and although I was becoming more fed up by the day, I wasn't sure how to leave him. So, when the abuse escalated, I completely stopped answering calls and cut everybody off including my family and best friend Stephanie. However, that was the worst thing that I could have done because no one could help protect me as I fought this battle on my own.

A Surprise Visit

It had been weeks since I had last answered Stephanie's calls. She knew all that had been going on until I stopped telling her things. She was becoming more opinionated about our relationship and I wasn't trying to hear how much she couldn't stand my boyfriend.

Maybe I told her too much, I thought. I was in love with Rashad and didn't know how to leave him.

But even ignored phone calls wasn't going to stop Stephanie from checking on me in other ways. So, like any best friend should, Stephanie made an unexpected visit to check on me.

***

I stayed at my apartment the whole day, trying to figure things out. I wasn't feeling like my normal self. I was depressed, but my pride wouldn't let me reach out for the help that I knew I needed. So, I turned off my phone ringer and lie in bed, stuck in my thoughts until they were interrupted by a knock at the door.

Who is that? I wondered, slightly perturbed. *I'm not expecting anyone.* I looked at my phone that had been faced down and on silent. There were a few missed calls, but I didn't expect anyone to come by.

Adjusting my robe, I walked towards the front door.

"Who is it?" I didn't have a peephole nor any other way to find out who was there.

"It's me," said the voice on the other side. "Girl open the door. Let me in."

I knew that voice. It was Stephanie.

I unlocked and opened the door to see her standing with a half-smile on her face while looking at me over her glasses. As usual, she welcomed herself in.

This heifer knows to call before coming over, I thought while closing the door behind her, but I didn't say nothing. I just let her walk in and say her piece.

"So, what's going on? You've been dodging all my calls and I wanna know why?" Stephanie eyed me suspiciously. She always gave me that "granny" look when she suspected juicy details. "And why are you wearing a robe in the middle of the day?" she asked snarkily.

I was not in the mood to be interrogated.

"Why do you keep checking on me," I asked with an attitude. "I'm fine. I'm okay. I'm just tired."

"Mmhmm," replied Stephanie eyeing me before looking around. "Where's Rashad?"

I groaned, rolled my eyes, and looked away before speaking in an agitated tone. "Why, Stephanie? So, you can tell me how much you don't like him?"

"You're my best friend, Jenesis and I want the best for you," her tone softened. "I know he's the reason why you haven't been answering my calls."

I looked away and stared blankly at the wall. She knew me, but if I told her what was going on for real, she would tell somebody and the last thing I wanted was for Rashad to go to jail. I felt like I could handle and fix the situation on my own.

"Look, I just wanted to see if you were okay," she said.

I slowly turned to face her, ready to defend myself and Rashad, but retreated on second thought, and gave her the silent treatment. I didn't know what to say. There were no words to say.

At the time, I thought she just didn't like Rashad for unknown reasons, but she was coming from a place of love. Stephanie was doing what was best for me— trying to help me and advocate on my behalf since I was keeping the abuse a secret.

Like Stephanie, Momma only knew so much. I was fearful of what would have happened to Rashad had she known the full extent of the relationship, not to mention what would happen if she shared it with anyone. I could only imagine my family's reaction had they known how toxic the relationship had become.

"I'm, okay," I reassured her. "I promise."

"You used to be so joyful and happy," said Stephanie. "Look at what he's doing to you. You're in here with the curtains pulled closed in this dark apartment. You don't even act the same. You can't tell me that you're happy."

Her words were beginning to soak through the numbness that consumed me.

"He ain't no good, Jenesis."

"I don't know what to do," I confessed, as my voice broke. "He's the closest thing that I have to my daughter."

Although I knew I didn't deserve the abuse, I felt like he was the only connection I had to Nadia. I also felt responsible for his wellbeing because I knew he was hurting just as much as I was. He just showed it differently.

However, rather than seeking help, I kept going back to what the women in my family referred to as the "same soup warmed over."

"Let him go," replied Stephanie.

"I don't know how," I admitted for the first time.

A Graveyard Relationship

Finally, I told Momma about the abuse. She was the last person I told, but she should have been the first. I knew how much she didn't like him, and this wouldn't help it.

"If you don't leave him, you will die," said Momma. "You're playing with fire, Jenesis."

We were in what Momma called a "graveyard relationship"— one that was bound by death. However, I ignored her warning.

"He loves me," I said trying to convince Momma through my tears, but she could see right through me. I was blinded by emotions and I wasn't thinking logically.

"Listen to me clearly, Jenesis," Momma said. "That boy don't love you. If he loved you, he wouldn't be putting his hands on you. Why are you doing this to yourself? Why do you keep allowing it? Do you love yourself? Because if you did, you wouldn't be putting up with all of this abuse. You don't deserve it."

As much as I hated hearing it, Momma was right. Even Ms. Katina, Rashad's Momma, pulled her son aside and talked to him.

"Stop putting your hands on that girl," she said. "What are you doing? Boy, what are you thinking?"

Both of our mothers were telling us the right thing to do. Rashad's Momma was telling him to stop hurting me. My Momma was telling me to leave him. But we both refused to listen.

"I just don't understand why you're allowing this. I didn't raise you this way," said Momma. She sighed and shook her head before continuing, "I'm trynna tell you, but I guess you're gonna have to learn the hard way."

I looked away and stared out the window. I wasn't sure how to face her. I kept so much hidden— I was ashamed and embarrassed. I wanted to tell Momma everything. I wanted help, but I just wasn't ready to speak out.

Why dont You understand

People dont understand
how my love forms for you.
People dont understand
Why I'm still with you
People dont understand
why you beat me
But I understand
even though you deceite me

Break the Stigma

While I coped with losing Nadia by going to school, Rashad went to the streets. He was practically playing Russian Roulette with his life and if he didn't leave the game soon, all bets would be off. He was used to the gamble. So, it wasn't long before Rashad got deeper into the streets in a way I never imagined.

Selling drugs was its own addiction that led into "using." It was a means to an end for his depression. He found, yet, another coping mechanism. He was a "pill popper," but he made sure to keep it hidden from me. The drug use heightened his aggressiveness and violent behavior. It was only a matter of time before things got worse.

At the time, I didn't know that Rashad was struggling with undiagnosed mental illness. The combination of mental illness and recreational drug use made Rashad a ticking time bomb. One minute he was happy and excited. The next, he was negative and depressed. While I noticed a change in his behavior, I never imagined that he was using drugs and still heavily engaged in crime. I didn't know to what extent Rashad was struggling with the loss of our daughter that he rarely talked about. He was stubborn. He could have gotten help, but he refused to admit that he needed it, so he went untreated. Rashad thought popping ecstasy, smoking weed, drinking alcohol, selling dope, and robbing people would help ease the pain, but it only made matters worse.

We both had our addictions. Rashad was my drug that I could always run back to—comfortable and dangerous. I wanted to help him get his life together. I wanted to fix his problems. I wanted to save him. But I couldn't do that. That was God's job.

During those dark times, I often recalled Momma's advice from when I lived back at home.

"You can lead a horse to water, but you can't make him drink," said Momma. Her words were like a bright light found in a dark tunnel.

As much as I wanted the best for Rashad, he didn't want to change. So, while his personal struggles went untreated, so did our relationship. Rashad feared losing me and I feared losing my life. We were both addicted without remedy.

Break the Generational Curse

The sweet young love that we once had all those summers under the city lights at the playground and by the railroad tracks were nothing but a memory. While I was growing into a mature, young college woman, Rashad was still in the streets and I was tired of it. We were not on the same page and I was beginning to question if we ever were.

The "street" image that appealed to me as a young, naïve girl, no longer thrilled me. I had outgrown Rashad's bad boy image. I wanted him to get his GED, go to trade school, and get an actual job, but he constantly resisted anything positive. We were at a crossroads and our relationship was becoming a train wreck.

Despite the abuse and its effects on my self-image and self-worth, I knew who I was, and I never lost sight of that. It took a while, but I finally felt ready to move on with my life and decided to break up with Rashad.

"We can't be together no more," I said trying to be strong.

That was the last thing Rashad wanted to hear. He snapped.

"You're not leaving me!" he said. "Don't ever say you're leaving me. Tell me you love me! Tell me!"

Before I could respond, Rashad rushed toward me, pinning me against the wall. He clasped his hands around my throat, choking me while staring into my eyes. He was soulless and empty. I couldn't breathe. I couldn't move. As soon as he released his grasp, I fell to the floor, crying. However, when Rashad saw my tears, he seemed to realize what he had done and snapped out of his belligerent state of mind. Sitting on the floor next to me, he spoke softly as if nothing had happened.

"Tell me you love me," he said with a strange calmness.

He reached to hold my hand, but I flinched in fear as he intertwined our fingers tightly. His grip was cold, weighty, and unwanted. I cried on the hardwood floors. I was weak, tired, and worn out. I wanted to leave the relationship, but I didn't know how to tell him without him getting angry. However, Rashad knew exactly what to say to make me feel guilty and pressured to stay with him.

"I can't live without you. I need you," he said as tears welled in his eyes.

What? I thought, perplexed. I lifted my head, looking at him in confusion as tears streamed down my face.

"If I can't have you, no one will," said Rashad. "Don't leave me."

Wiping my face, I looked at him and felt sorry. I fell for it every time.

He loves me, I thought. *He's just going through a lot, right now. He didn't mean to put his hands on me.*

"I love you," I expressed to Rashad as I wiped my tears away.

It was manipulation. Rashad had flipped the script. I forgot all about what he had done wrong and once again put his needs before my own. I loved him. I didn't want nothing bad to happen to him. I was scared. I was in love. But I was tired. My eyes hurt from crying. My stomach burned from heaving. My limbs ached from fighting. All that was left were bruises seen and unseen.

Why cant I see?
Why do you look in my eyes
to hear my story.
Why did you find my heart
to find my glory.
Why do you kiss me so
that I wont let go.
I finally found out
what it was all about
Your soul was with me
Your heart was too
but it was too late
I had already lost you.

Busted

What kind of love leaves bruises? This was a thought that constantly went through my mind.

There was one morning in particular when an accusation turned into a full-fledged fight that led to the destruction of items around my apartment. Damaging things that mattered to me was one of the ways that he tried to control and manipulate me.

In fits of rage, Rashad always grabbed my cell phone. Without a phone, I couldn't call family, the police, or anyone for that matter. I couldn't get any help whatsoever. These phones were thrown in the river, smashed on the ground, launched into an open field— you name it— it happened. And that wasn't all. Items around my apartment were destroyed, clothing was torn, glass was broken, and pictures were scratched out and defaced.

With no phone and protection, I felt helpless. Rashad kept yelling and grabbing on me, so I fought back the best way I could until I couldn't hold my own anymore. I grabbed a Louisville Slugger baseball bat from behind my closet to defend myself. I didn't want to hit him, but if I had to protect myself, I would.

"If you don't stop, I will hit you!" I threatened with the bat in my hands. "Get out!" I screamed.

But that was the last thing that Rashad wanted. He wrestled me down to the floor, stood over me, pried the bat out of my hands, and began to threaten me with it.

"Stop!" I yelled, holding my hands up in defense. "Please, stop!"

I wasn't sure if he would hit me with the bat or not. I thought he loved me, but I also knew his anger was out of control. I didn't put anything past him. But, thankfully, my neighbors heard the commotion, called the police, and in a matter of minutes, my front door was kicked in by two cops.

One wrestled Rashad down, handcuffed, placed him under arrest, and escorted him to the cop car in only boxers and a T-shirt. The other cop brought his jeans out— the same jeans that had four grams in "dimes" ($10 worth of crack) and "dub pieces" ($20 worth of crack) that were bagged up in one of his pockets.

Unknowingly, the police officer put the jeans on Rashad without checking the pockets. However, while handcuffed in the backseat, Rashad found a way to dig into his pocket and swallow the crack. If he hadn't, he would have been facing trafficking charges and a longer prison sentence.

This was Rashad's first domestic violence arrest, and one of many incidents that would cause him to get locked-up. However, it would take multiple police visits to my apartment, countless arguments, furious fights, and innumerable tears for something to change.

The Break Up

Rashad was sentenced to five months in jail, but even then, we stayed in the relationship. However, while we tried to work things out, our relationship wasn't getting any better. So, a few weeks after Rashad was released from jail, I was ready to call it quits— for real, this time.

"It's over," I told Rashad. "I want you to leave."

I could see in his face that he was crushed and disappointed, but not surprised.

"Why?" he asked, apprehensively. "I can't live without you."

"I'm not interested in doing this anymore," I said, for the first time with conviction. I needed to be strong. I needed Rashad to know that I was serious. I couldn't show any sign of weakness. This time, I wasn't giving him another chance.

"I'm tired of going through these fights," I confessed.

But Rashad wasn't hearing me. He thought that in order for me to leave, there had to be another man involved. He was wrongfully accusing me of cheating, yet again. He just couldn't accept the truth— that I didn't want to be with him anymore because he was abusive.

Instead of understanding where I was coming from, Rashad's insecurities got the best of him. His mood quickly switched from sadness to anger as he screamed, grabbed, pushed, and pulled on me.

"I don't want to be with you anymore!" I screamed. "I can't keep going through this with you. Just leave me alone!"

Hearing those words made him angrier. I wasn't going anywhere if he had anything to do with it. At least, that's how he saw it.

Furious, he snatched my phone from my hands and threw it across the room, breaking it into pieces.

"So, you're gonna leave me?!" Rashad yelled.

Rushing towards me, he pinned me against the wall, and held my arms above my head while cussing and calling me out of my name.

"Let me go!" I screamed, trying to break free. "Get off of me! I will call the police on you! Get your hands off of me!"

Squirming, I was able to loosen his grasp and escape from the apartment, but no matter how fast I ran, Rashad always caught me.

"You're not leaving me!" he screamed. "You're gonna have to kill me first!"

That Night

A few days later, Rashad called my phone the whole day, but I ignored his calls. It was the day before my big psychology exam and I needed to concentrate and study. My grades had suffered because of our fights, and I really needed to get my act together, if I planned on keeping my full academic scholarship.

My grades weren't the only thing that suffered either. I was mentally, emotionally, spiritually, and physically drained. It had only been a few months of my first semester in college and I was already failing tests, but this particular exam had the power to either make or break me. I couldn't afford to fail this final test. So, I turned off the ringer to my cell phone and placed it face down on my bed to study in peace and quiet.

While studying, I managed to fall asleep until I heard a loud noise that jolted me awake.

Boom!

The front door to my apartment was kicked in and the chair that I had lodged under the door knob for extra protection (a result of a previous break-in by Rashad) was gone. I thought I was dreaming until I saw a large black shadow standing outside of my glass French doors to my bedroom.

In a frenzy, I sat up in bed and pulled the covers over my body, but, Rashad had already opened my bedroom doors, grabbing me from the bed and dragging me across the floor into the kitchen.

"Get your fucking hands off me!" I screamed, swinging at him in self-defense.

"I fucking hate you, you bitch!" he yelled.

Grabbing my forearms, he pinned me against the refrigerator, so that I couldn't move, and that's when he hacked up a wad of phlegm from the back of his throat and repeatedly spat in my face. I squeezed my eyes closed and struggled to escape his grasp while shaking my head to escape his venom. I had never been so disrespected and disgusted in my life.

Loosening his strong hold, I dropped to the floor and vigorously wiped my face as best as I could. But Rashad's madness intensified. Holding me down with one hand, he grabbed a knife from the kitchen drawer, put it to his throat, and wrapped my hand around the knife handle.

"Kill me!" he yelled. "Kill me, then kill yourself so we can be with our baby in heaven." Tears streamed down his face.

"Get off of me!" I screamed, straining to pull my hand away from him.

"You stupid bitch! I hate you!" he yelled, choking me against the refrigerator.

Squealing, I bucked my arms free from his grasp, snatched my hand away from the knife, and ran out of the apartment.

Rashad followed me until I ran into a nearby dry cleaners to get help and call the police. But, by the time they arrived, Rashad was gone. He had become a monster and a shadow in my life.

I had this man's child and he did this to me? All I could do was cry into my hands. I was in utter disbelief.

A New Start

I was in love with a monster. It would take angels of faith and sacrifice to leave Rashad. I was still holding on to what I knew—an abusive relationship that continued until Rashad was locked up for another warrant.

Even after his second stint in jail, we stayed in contact through phone calls, written letters, and visitation days.

During those visits, we talked through a window from a corded phone that reminded me of past visits to see Daddy Kyle who had been locked up in prison for over four years. However, even in jail, Rashad made false cheating accusations that left me storming out of the visitation room on a few occasions.

I was beginning to imagine what life would be like without Rashad. I was thinking about moving on. So, the first thing I thought to do was exactly that— move.

Rashad will soon be on work release from jail and I need a fresh start at a new apartment, I thought.

However, even though we were still together, off and on, I wasn't going to tell him where I lived.

"I'm moving," I professed to Momma. "I'm done with Rashad."

She was relieved and thankful that I was beginning to listen.

"Don't let your choices be in vain, Jenesis," Momma said. "Don't go back."

"I can't go through this anymore," I told Momma as I sat thinking about everything.

It hurt to know that Rashad and I could never be what we had always hoped for. It just wasn't in God's plan, but I still didn't know how to accept that.

The Final Straw

I moved into my second apartment and for the first time, I didn't feel anxious, scared, worried, or on-edge. I felt safe and secure. However, that didn't last long.

After numerous phone calls and messages, I gave into Rashad's pleas to see me and be together and invited him over to my new apartment. But just like clockwork and any other time, Rashad's demons showed up, causing me to flee and call Stephanie.

When she arrived, Rashad had already fled the scene. I was left bruised and battered.

"I should have left a long time ago," I cried to Stephanie while sitting in her car. "I should have never invited him over here. I just can't believe this."

"Believe it," said Stephanie. "He's crazy."

In order to love myself again, I needed to let go of Rashad. I was only hurting myself by staying. However, while I didn't know how to let go, Stephanie did.

"I know exactly what you need to do," said Stephanie. "We're going down to the courthouse so that you can file an EPO (Emergency Protection Order)."

I looked at Stephanie and saw the look on her face. She was not playing. I wasn't sure if I was ready to go that far.

"If you stay with him, don't tell me nothing else about him," said Stephanie. "I'm serious, Jenesis."

As I sat silent, I saw the hurt in her eyes. She genuinely loved and cared for me.

"You don't deserve to be treated like this," she said. "This is craziness. If you don't tell on him, then I will."

I felt hopeless as fear swept over me. I didn't want anything bad to happen to Rashad, but at the same time, he was hurting me. It was time for me to come to terms with the reality that our relationship was over.

"Take me downtown to the courthouse," I said firmly while staring into the street traffic.

"Are you sure?"

"Yes," I replied.

"You ain't said nothing but a word," said Stephanie.

And just like that, we were headed downtown to the courthouse to file a Domestic Violence Order (DVO) and EPO. It was time for me to do my part and get justice for myself, so I filed the paperwork and had photos taken of my bruises.

Case Closed

June 6th. The time had come for me to stand before the judge in the courtroom for the domestic violence case that I had filed against Rashad. He had been in jail for nearly a month and I was regretful for having filed the order. I felt at fault and to blame for his status as an inmate. Now, he was potentially facing a longer sentence— in prison.

As I sat in the courtroom, encircled by women advocates, Rashad entered through a side door from the back-holding cell wearing an orange jumpsuit with his wrists handcuffed in front of him. He stood between the judge and a police officer, looking from me to the floor. Shame and sadness sat deep in his eyes.

If I never told Stephanie, I wouldn't be in this situation, I thought, remorseful. *I should have never said anything.*

However, what I failed to realize at the time was that it wasn't Stephanie's fault or mine that Rashad was sentenced to. It was Rashad's actions who got him in this predicament.

Although, the women advocates encouraged me to speak out and tell the judge everything that had happened, before I approached the stand, all of my courage diminished. Instead of defending for myself, I pleaded to the judge on Rashad's behalf.

"Please, just give him less time," I begged the judge who stared at me stoically.

"I can help him. I know he can change," I said. "Please, Your Honor, just give him another chance."

I was protecting Rashad and supporting his abusive behaviors by not speaking up for myself. However, as I pleaded, I didn't know that this was the same judge who had given Rashad several chances to get his life right in the past. He was already on probation from a dope case he caught two years prior, and since then, he had stood in the same courtroom and in front of the same judge for three other domestic violence cases from our relationship. He pleaded guilty to one and the other two were dropped. He also faced other charges— possession of marijuana, an escape, a theft by unlawful taking over $1,000, and fleeing the police. It would take a lot of convincing for Rashad to get off this time.

The judge stared at me expressionless before speaking, "I want you to take a real good look at him."

I turned toward Rashad, looking into his hopeless and careless eyes. He stood at the stand, unraveling in every way, from his unkept cornrows to his freedom, and from his dignity to our relationship. This was a man who I loved unconditionally, no matter the struggles. But today, he looked different.

"Listen to me," said the judge. "You have a chance. You are in college on a full scholarship. Focus on school."

I wasn't hearing her and continued pleading to the judge.

"Please, just give him one last chance," I said. "I love him, and I know he can change."

And that's when the judge looked me in my face and spoke crystal clear.

"He ain't neva' gon' change, baby girl," said the judge. "Motion to revoke sustained."

The judge picked up the gavel and hit it against the sound block. Case closed.

Rashad's dropped his chin to his chest, shaking his head.

I felt powerless. I had lost Nadia. Now, I was losing the closest thing to her— her father. But he wasn't just going to jail or a work release program. This time, he was going to prison for two years.

As the police officer escorted Rashad out of the courtroom and back to the holding cell, he lifted his head and held it high. I knew, internally, he felt he was at his lowest, similar to when Nadia passed, but he just couldn't show any sign of emotion. He was in a jungle among other criminals.

Walking out of the courtroom, I held in my tears, stuck in the privacy of my thoughts. *I should have never told*, I thought. I felt guilty for the consequences that Rashad faced even though the abuse was not my fault.

After exiting the building, tears tumbled down my face like leaves during Autumn as my thoughts consumed me. *Now, I don't have him anymore. I don't have nobody.*

At the time, I didn't understand why things happened the way they did. All I could do was pray, but God knows best.

Part SEVEN

Hope & Healing

Wise Words

Listen to me closely, Jenesis. The only way that you are going to heal is through forgiveness. Forgiveness is not about the person who did you wrong. It's about you. It's about your healing. End the cycle of abuse today. You have to know when to pull away and let go, baby. Get rid of the dust. Unpack the bag. Get out of that box and step outside of your comfort zone. If the person can't grow with you, then they can't go with you. Don't accept no wooden nickels, you hear me? And always remember that your struggle is your strength and your pain is your purpose. Keep going and never stop following your dreams. No matter what you go through, understand that your path is your choice. Be careful who you attract. Be cautious when entering new relationships. Be all that God's called you to be. And don't you ever lose sight of that.

A Butterfly

For months after Rashad was sentenced to prison, we tried to stay in touch as much as we possibly could. Collect phone calls and mailed letters made the transition of him going to prison and us holding on to what we once had, more feasible.

However, our relationship was too toxic for us to stay together. The mere thought of staying in a relationship with someone who was abusive to me just didn't make any sense. So, when I unexpectedly didn't hear from him for months at a time due to bad behavior in prison that sent him to isolation with no contact, I began to reevaluate everything about our relationship including Rashad, my well-being, and my future. I knew that it was time to let go.

The time that I had apart from Rashad, helped me come to terms with the fact that our love would never be the way that it had once been all those summers ago. I was finally ready to walk away from Rashad. I sent him a final letter to end the relationship and stopped accepting his calls and returning his letters. Just like Momma and Daddy Kyle, our relationship had run its course and there was no turning back.

Enough is enough, I repeatedly told myself to reaffirm my decision and not fall back into old habits of staying in the relationship. I was ready to let go and grow.

forgiveness

it took him years to smile

he never forgot
the way her palm rested in his

he never forgot
the aroma of her showered body
before breakfast

he never forgot
her busy schedule
and endless kisses before dusk

he never forgot
how alone he felt
after she stopped smiling

he never forgot
how she left their home
a key, laying on the pillow

he has forgotten how to love again
and it is taking him many years
to smile and to forget

Transformation

It was my second year in college when me and Rashad's relationship officially ended, and we went our separate ways. During that time, I shifted my attention to school. A mother's heart had grown inside of me for over nine months and led me to explore my gifts, aspirations, and goals. So, it was only natural that I poured my heart and soul back into writing.

Without the headache and heartache of an unhealthy relationship, my life as a college student led me down a path that I never imagined. I studied abroad internationally, spearheaded a campus publication, joined a sorority, and started to build the life that I always dreamed of living. I was on a road to success— determined that nothing, or no one would stop me from walking in my purpose.

Finally, I can spread my wings and soar, I thought.

I was finding God and myself. And I had found poetry.

Two Years Later

December 19th. Two years had passed when I received the free call from VINE (Victim Information and Notification Everyday) notifying me of Rashad's prison release date. He had served his sentence and would soon be free. Shortly, after receiving the automated call, seconds later, another call came through.

My cell phone buzzed, but when I saw "unknown" flash across the screen, I knew it was Rashad. He was calling me collect from Union State Reformatory.

Since deciding to finally leave Rashad for good, I was focused on school, traveling internationally, and in a new relationship. I had moved on. However, while the tears had been wiped away and the bruises had faded, the internal scars and pain were still there.

Three Years After

I took the pain onto another continent. Wooden
springs. Never had you been there. Had you felt
these pains kept numb in my veins. Formation of
words could not tell me of the 1:05 early. No
one listened. Deaf ears ironed into the fabric.
Neither could protect me; wipe away the drain in
the bridge of my nose. Joy could have, come.
God passed his angels through the rain. Two
rooms. One deceased. Release from fallopian
tube and brain. Body shifted insanely. From
their lips, syllables became real before the room
changed.

Hot blankets draped. Neck and feet with fever
rush. Could not hunger liquid or eat. Wet
pillows willow and cascade into hands in secret
for onlookers. In memory of better day. Smooth
sharp stories for them. Disrupted. Delayed is my
own. To meet what's left of fresh face lines.
Searching trademark of my presence. Dimples.
Grace. Tresses. In linen and lace. Her body
changed by day although I prayed. I mothered
her. With my lips, I smothered her. Told she
would never speak. Never would she blink. No
matter what, she was mine. My baby. Her body

was still. Breasts leaking with mother's milk.
Held onto baby until body began to sink.

My baby was taken from me. And, covered with
a veil on ice. Four days. For days unlike this. I
knew I had failed. A derailed assignment. But
rise. Not for you. Rise. Just for two. Rise. You
must prove. It took 5 days. Bedridden moves. It
took many layers to remove the shedding skin.
Become anew. To fill flower funeral. To walk
across that stage with diploma in hand into black
cloud smoke. To bring my child's face to the
stage.

From the stands, the camera zooms. Beat the
odds this young girl bruised beaten with strength
in pieces in particles. Daddy is behind stone that
won't grant words a touch a feeling a blockade
of walls and blankets that shutter speed breathe
from her life. From the stands, the camera
zooms. To various places that don't hold her like
baby hands and new love. Never finding what
she is really looking for. Strolling. Scrolling
through limitless thank you's and memory cards.
All broken. But never full. Too full. Pain and
Glory. Never too full.

.

Freedom

Three generations of women sat on the couch in the living room— me, Grandma, and Momma. That's where wisdom came from— places I called home.

"Love is patient. Love is kind," Grandma read from her Bible. "That's 1 Corinthians 13: 4-8."

Momma reaffirmed Grandma's words. "You're gonna be just fine," said Momma. "God told me when I was pregnant with you: 'Everything's going to be okay' and for me not to worry."

The storm was difficult, but I survived. I learned many lessons with the most paramount being— love doesn't hurt; love heals, and that sometimes you have to let go of some things in order to grow into your fullest potential.

I was preparing for my metamorphosis. The road to healing was long, but I understood that I needed to turn my pain into my purpose and my struggle into my strength. This realization allowed me to become the woman that I am today.

A Letter from Rashad

Jenesis,

  Despite what we went through, you still accepted me. Even when I was locked up in county, you wrote me whenever you could and sent pictures. You didn't have to, but you did. But when I got to prison, I knew things would change. You was in college. I was in prison. Being locked away from everyone— those were some of the darkest hours of my life. I wanted to end my life, but I knew I still had you, my sister, and my Momma who loved me.

  Despite all that I put you through, you still loved me and was there for me. I didn't deserve you. I didn't treat you right. I just didn't know how long I would have you in my life. And that was what I feared the most. I really do apologize for not knowing how to control my anger. When I abused you, I never thought that I was hurting you. I was raised around stuff like that. I wasn't punching or slapping you, so I felt like what I was doing weren't signs of abuse. But I was wrong, and I eventually had to learn the hard way.

  Lord knows that I'm sorry for abusing you. I'm not the same person I was at 18 years-old. Who was I to put my hands on you? I never should have disrespected you. There are no excuses for what I did and I take full responsibility for my actions. I could never tell you enough how sorry I am for the pain that I caused you. You didn't deserve that. No woman deserves that. You're the first person that ever accepted me for me. You didn't judge me. When you were ready to go, I should have let you. But instead, I didn't know how to let go.

Growing up, I was laughed at and misjudged. That was until I learned how to fight. But when I was with you, I could let my guard down and feel happy. I didn't have to put on a tough demeanor around you. I wanted to show you that I loved you. I just didn't know how. I was too broken to show it. I couldn't enjoy the happiest of moments with you because I was so afraid of losing you. I wasn't what I thought you wanted. I always thought you wanted someone else and my insecurities got the best of me. My thoughts held me back. But today, I stand as a man and it feels so good to be the man that I am today. Thank you for always being there for me and believing in me. You've helped me more than you could ever know, and for that, I will forever love you and be grateful for you.

-Rashad

A Letter to Jenesis

Through all of the pain and struggle, the Lord taught me a lesson. Nadia's life and legacy are a testimony of hope, healing, faith, and forgiveness through God. At the time, I didn't see the blessing. I didn't understand why I was chosen to go through that. I was in the eye of a storm. However, if I had not experienced these storms, I would not have learned to survive in them. With pain comes purpose and with struggle comes strength.

It took from May 19, 2005 to May 19, 2019 for this to all cool off before the story was told.

On Mother's Day, I am now done writing. I am sitting on my bed, unpacking the red luggage bag from the hospital all those years ago. I am releasing the pain and allowing my purpose to flow in remembrance of Nadia's precious spirit that will forever live on in my heart.

Love,

Tykanna

13 Years Later...

Present Day

True story.

Rashad and Jenesis' relationship started and ended at the train tracks. Hip Hop was on one side. Poetry was on the other. And while you may say beat and rhyme go hand in hand, and that you can't have one without the other, music has the power to either bring people together or tear them apart. They were destined to go down two different paths from the beginning. They say, the way you meet someone, can also be the same way you lose them.

Rashad stayed in the streets for years, until he decided to leave them behind for good. However, it would take several drug busts, run-ins with the police, and jail time before he finally made a change to turn his life around. He eventually earned his GED, acquired a trade, pursued his music career, and built a comfortable life for himself.

Jenesis stayed in school and used her love as a mother and passion as a writer to travel internationally as a poet/spoken word artist, motivational speaker, launch a book publishing and entertainment company, and pursue a PhD in Education (Curriculum & Instruction). She has published over seven books that she teaches from to intergenerational communities worldwide.

Truth be told, Rashad and Jenesis' love was young and premature. And while some things last a lifetime, others are only for a season. Either way, there is a lesson to learn from Rashad and Jenesis' urban love story that is— well, definitely one to remember.

Behind my Skin

Fourteen years ago today

from the city bus window in a midnight hour
my hopes and dreams and plans are all growing
inside of me

i am pregnant. i hide things under my skin.
embryo kicks my eyes open. fetus hiccups
during math tests. lecture class about my plans.
to tell my story. but i am embarrassed. shame
grips my baby waist. this child is innocent. from
the things that makes me human. child dont
deserve to repent. baby fingers and toes press
and push against the silent earth inside me. for
loud noise i cant hear yet. is a long revealing
lesson i must soon face.

this one gon be tough, they say.

i clutch this child in my womb.
want her to see the mother she belongs to.
carried her nine months warm breathing.
held her four days cold breathless

it's the birthday of another child somewhere in
the world breasts throb full and pull from a body
that wasn't prepared to be a mother just so soon
heart pours from new and unfamiliar vacant
pores that ache slowly
but i must smile,
hug
and thank the people who brought flowers to the
funeral and filled the water pitcher.
and, prepare for all that lies ahead of me
all that i am and to become
woman. wife. mother. daughter. sister. artist.
writer. student. doctor. teacher
but at the end of the day
i am all that the earth will have me to be.

so, fourteen years ago, today

i'd tell that girl whose face sits illuminated
in the city bus window
whose hopes and dreams and plans are all
growing inside of her
don't you dare give up now

it's gon be tough but
so are you

When Hip Hop Met Poetry

Massage through this beat
Give this story
time- attention it deserves
Come flow with me
Come flow with me

Beginning
True story
Real life
Romeo and Juliet.
Real talk
Bonnie and Clyde.
That crazy kind of love
Crazy kind of love

we were laid up
teenage youth
poverty-infested room
with the whole world
against us

our family at war

we made a baby
we had a child
she was born

the peace treaty

streetlights
secrets
payphones
Runaway
love

you dodged the bullets
and
had
the shells
to prove it
piss- liquor stained stairwells
opened every door for you

that homeless
unbreakable
limitless
dangerous
fearless
kind of love

hospital
sterile
lifeless
born still.
just too good for this here hurting world

Held in our arms
four days
held in our hearts
four seasons
held in our memories

Innumerable
unmeasurable
tears ago

I gave you
two angels.
One named
faith
the second,
named
sacrifice

"For I know the plans I have for you...plans to
prosper you and not to harm you, plans to give
you hope and a future."

orange jumpsuit
shackled at the wrist
you still had my heart
in the arms of women advocates
you still had my heart
even after all the pain

you still had my heart

"He ain't never gone change,
baby girl"

grant him less time
spare his life
the wound is deep
we can't make this right
gambled it all
But was it worth the fight
Integrity is one thing
i just won't compromise

i-was-there
loved you
more-than-myself
endured the worst days
loved you
more-than-myself
normalized dysfunction

I will never love another
more than myself

we couldn't love
the right way
tried to give me the world

the right way
give me your heart
the right way
can only
give what you previously own
the right way

what kind of love leaves bruises?
I bled for you
went through hell and back
trauma
tragedy
I made it through

you
lost me
to college

I
lost you
to prison

you
hung pictures
in your cell
confinement
conviction

I traveled the world
purpose passion driven
poetic-verse
spoken
word
on a mission

"You can make plans,
but the Lord's purpose will prevail."

wise woman once told me
dig up the roots
there's recovery-healing
when you inspect the fruit
damage
brokenness
an internal seed
you have two options:
heal-hurt
evolve-repeat

and forgiveness,
forgiveness is love
redemption
reconciliation
repentance

struggle is strength...

made
me
the
woman
I
am
today

About the Author

I am 13 years of age, in the 8th grade living in Louisville ky

My favorite poem writer's are: Maya Angelou, Tytianna Wells, + Tionne Watkins.

message - The author of its book is Tytianna N.M. Wells. I was born in Detroite MI. And raised in Louisville ky. I lived a tough life but when I got hurt I would read, write poetry or a story, listen to music or just go to sleep

About the Author

Tytianna Nikia Maria Wells is an author, illustrator, publisher, producer, professor, and motivational speaker. She has published seven books. She has also released a spoken word song and wrote and directed a short film for her first memoir, *When Hip Hop Met Poetry: An Urban Love Story.*

Tytianna holds a dual Bachelor of Arts degree in English and Pan-African Studies, and a Master of Arts degree in Pan-African Studies. She is pursuing a PhD in Education (Curriculum & Instruction) at the University of Louisville. She is the recipient of numerous scholarships, fellowships, and grants. Tytianna enjoys spending time with family, traveling the world, and empowering the community. She lives in Louisville, Kentucky.